W9-BSD-217

Folktales

in

Homer's *Odyssey*

The Carl Newell Jackson Lectures · *1972*

Folktales

in

Homer's *Odyssey* .

Lionel

Denys Page

Harvard University Press

Cambridge, Massachusetts

1973

ROCKINGHAM PUBLIC LIBRARY
HARRISONBURG, VIRGINIA 22801

883.01
P

© Copyright 1973 by the President and Fellows of Harvard College
All rights reserved
Library of Congress Catalog Card Number 73–75056
SBN 674–30720–8
Printed in the United States of America

Preface

The first four chapters of this book reproduce the Carl Newell Jackson Lectures delivered at Harvard University in April 1972. The Appendix is a slightly modified version of a lecture delivered in Athens in 1963 and published in the Ἐπιστημονικὴ Ἐφημερὶς τῆς Φιλοσοφικῆς Σχολῆς τοῦ Πανεπιστημίου Ἀθηνῶν, 1964; I have often been asked to make it more generally accessible, and I now take advantage of Professor N. Kondoleon's kind permission to do so.

To my hosts at Harvard, and especially to Professor George Goold, I offer most cordial thanks for great personal kindness and generous hospitality to my wife and myself.

Denys Page

Contents

Folktales

in

Homer's *Odyssey*

I

The
Lotus-Eaters

I Early in the ninth book of the *Odyssey* Odysseus begins the description of the perils which he had survived on the way from Troy to Phaeacia, his last stage before arrival home in Ithaca.[1] Several of the names first heard in this narrative have been household words ever since: the Lotus-Eaters; Cyclops, the one-eyed giant; Circe, the beautiful witch; the Sirens; Scylla and Charybdis; Calypso. I doubt if any part of ancient poetry has given greater pleasure; and there is a particular and obvious reason for this. Here, as very seldom elsewhere in Greek literature, we find ourselves in the enchanting land of folktale,[2] among giants and ogres and monsters and magicians and beautiful ladies half-divine. The poet's voice is as the nightingale's:

> The same that oft-times hath
> Charm'd magic casements, opening on the foam
> Of perilous seas, in faery lands forlorn.

The appeal of folktale is universal. Stories of this kind have always and everywhere enthralled the listener, from infancy to old age; and in this part of the *Odyssey* we find a number of the most popular of such tales up-lifted to the highest peak of poetry.

The stories told are as follows, in order: (1) a raid on the coast of Thrace; (2) the Lotus-Eaters; (3) Cyclops, the one-eyed ogre; (4) Aeolus and his bag of winds; (5) the Laestrygonians, giants and cannibals; (6) Circe; (7) the visit to the Underworld; (8) the Sirens; (9) the Wandering Rocks and Scylla and Charybdis; (10) the holy Cattle of the Sun. By this time Odysseus has lost all his companions; the story ends with his arrival at the island of Calypso.

These tales occupy four books of the *Odyssey*, about 2,200 lines, over one-sixth of the poem. It should be

3

understood that the folktale element in this part is not out of harmony with the poem as a whole. The theme of the *Odyssey* itself is an adaptation of a folktale—the common and widespread tale[3] of the husband who returns home after many years; finds that his wife has been faithful despite trials and temptations; and is now so changed in appearance that he must prove his identity by tests and tokens.

Nevertheless, although harmonious in principle, the folktales in these four books called for careful handling in detail. The story of the *Odyssey* as a whole is based on folktale, but that folktale is adapted to persons believed to be historical. It is consequently set in the real world, and blended with past and present realities. Supernatural elements are, for the most part, either suppressed or so modified as to seem credible. The world of the *Odyssey* is largely a world within the experience and knowledge, or at least the belief, of its audience. The persons are lifelike, and so are most of the events; of those which are not, most are so treated as to seem acceptable, or at least not wholly incredible, to the listener in the Dark Age of Greece and later.

This illusion might easily have been destroyed by the introduction of a long parade of well-known figures of common folktale, such as one-eyed ogres and sorceresses turning men into pigs with a stroke of the wand. We may quite often notice, in passing, the care taken by the poet to suppress or at least to modify the magical elements in the folktales which he adapts, and to represent even such tales as these as though they were almost, if not quite, within the bounds of reality.

The ten stories in these four books are by no means all of the same type. The first adventure differs in kind from all the others; and the difference is plainly intentional. The story of the adventures has begun, and first impressions are important. So here, at the start, is a wholly realistic raid on the coast of Thrace, a place we all know, against the Kikones, a people we have all heard about.[4] Our passage to the remoter world of Lotus-Eaters and the like is made as easy as may be, and the illusion of reality created by this first adventure is to be maintained so far as possible; it is never to be wholly dispelled, seldom to be obscured.

I have spoken of folktale as the source of the following stories; not, as I shall try to show, altogether truly. The true nature of some of the stories is not what it seems; the motifs of some are much closer to real life than you may have supposed.

So first, the curious episode of the Lotus-Eaters.

Odyssey 9.80–104: Odysseus and his companions set sail from the coast of Thrace. Their course lay down the east coast of the Peloponnese, round its southern promontories, and up the west coast to Ithaca: 'But as I was doubling Cape Malea, the waves and current and northwind drove me off course and drifted me away from Cythera. From there, for nine days I was swept over the fishy sea by ruinous winds; and on the tenth we landed in the country of the Lotus-Eaters, who live on a food of flowers. There we set foot on the mainland and drew water, and my companions quickly took their dinner beside the swift ships. When we had tasted of food and drink, I sent some of my company to inquire what sort of men ate their bread in the country. I chose two men, and gave them a third for company as spokesman. So they went and very soon were in the midst of men who were Lotus-Eaters. Now the Lotus-Eaters did not plan to kill my companions, but gave them lotus to taste.

And when anyone of them ate the honeysweet fruit of the lotus, he no longer wished to bring a message back, or to return, but wanted to stay there and feed on lotus among the Lotus-Eaters, and to forget about going home. I myself brought them weeping to the ships by force, and dragged them under the rowing-benches and tied them up in the hollow ships. And I commanded my other trusty companions to make haste and embark in the swift ships, fearing that someone else might eat of the lotus and forget about going home. They quickly embarked and sat on the benches, and sitting in order smote the gray water with their oars'.

Here is very little said about the Lotus-Eaters. They ate lotus; they meant you no harm; they gave you lotus to eat, and you wanted to stay with them for ever. That is all: and for the rest of time nobody has ever known anything more about the Lotus-Eaters. For hundreds of years geographers argued about their location, botanists debated what sort of lotus they ate. But if we look for other facts about them, we must wait almost a thousand years from the time of Herodotus, when Stephanus of Byzantium will publish his great geographical dictionary. There, under the entry Γέρμαρα, we read a cryptic notice: the Germara are 'a Celtic people, who do not see the sunlight; as Aristotle says in his book *On Wonderful Things*, "the Lotus-Eaters sleep for six months"'.[5] This is the only new thing ever said about the Lotus-Eaters; it is plainly fiction, and the alleged authority is bogus. Aristotle was not the author of the book *On Wonderful Things to Hear*, περὶ θαυμασίων ἀκουσμάτων; nor in fact does that collection of improbabilities say anything about Lotus-Eaters, asleep or waking.

There is nothing particularly surprising in the fact that

the *Odyssey* contains the only information about the Lotus-Eaters that was ever known to any post-Homeric Greek. What I find surprising is the fact that this episode, which has a certain charm, made no impact on the imagination of the poetical and romantic writers of Greece and Rome. Nor is it represented in Greek or Roman art. There is nothing but brief allusion, and even that is rare. Not counting geographers and botanists, I reckon about a dozen brief allusions in Greek from Xenophon to Palladas, not so many in Latin from Cicero to Ammianus.[6] Only from the dismal soul of the mythographer Hyginus,[7] in the second century A.D., was wrung a rare cry. Dullest of mortals, he has the unique distinction, among the ancients, of being emotionally aroused when he contemplates the Lotus-Eaters: *Lotophagos*, he cries, *homines minime malos*; 'they were really very good people'. This is not much, but it is something; it is an ember aglow in the ash-heap. Warm your hands while you may, for it will be long enough before you find another.

From the eighth century B.C. up to the year A.D. 1832 the Lotus-Eaters lived only in the *Odyssey*. Then the heart of Lord Tennyson was moved by these lines of Homer, and he published *The Lotos-Eaters*, a poem which has the atmosphere of a steamy hot-house overfilled with exotic odorous blooms; some very beautiful, some drooping and faded, but altogether heavy-scented and enervating.

Odysseus and his companions reach the land of the Lotus-Eaters:

> In the afternoon they came unto a land
> In which it seemed always afternoon ...

.   .   .

A land where all things always seemed the same;
And round about the keel with faces pale,
Dark faces pale against that rosy flame,
The mild-eyed melancholy Lotos-Eaters came.
Branches they bore of that enchanted stem,
Laden with flower and fruit, whereof they gave
To each, but those who did receive of them,
And taste, to him the gushing of the wave
Far, far away did seem to mourn and rave
On alien shores; and if his fellow spake,
His voice was thin, as voices from the grave;
And deep-asleep he seemed, yet all awake,
And music in his ears his beating heart did make.

    They sat them down upon the yellow sand
Between the sun and moon upon the shore;
And sweet it was to dream of Fatherland,
Of child, and wife, and slave; but evermore
Most weary seem'd the sea, weary the oar,
Weary the wandering fields of barren foam.
Then some one said, 'We will return no more';
And all at once they sang, 'Our island home
Is far beyond the wave; we will no longer roam'.

No such romantic note is struck by the ancients. They have no interest in the Lotus-Eaters, except to inquire just where they lived and what they ate.

Locating the Lotus-Eaters has been for many the pastime of idle hours, from Herodotus to the present day. Herodotus[8] placed them in Tripolitania, as western neighbours of the Gindánes, whose women (he says) wear many ankle-bracelets of leather, one for each lover; and the woman with the greatest number of anklets is thought to be the best woman, as being the most loved. Now (he continues) 'there is a headland jutting out to sea from the land of these Gindánes. It is inhabited by Lotus-Eaters, who live by eating nothing but the fruit of the lotus. The fruit of the lotus is the size of the mastich-berry, similar in sweetness to the fruit of the date-palm. The Lotus-Eaters make wine of it too'.

The geographical position is clear enough, because the eastern neighbours of the Lotus-Eaters, the Machlyes, are bounded on the west by an identifiable feature, Lake Tritonis.[9] So the Lotus-Eaters lived (roughly speaking) on the North African coast facing *Syrtis Minor*.

I shall not repeat the variations on this theme composed by later geographers.[10] There is a choice between various points on, and islands off, the coast of North Africa from Morocco to Cyrene. Or you might find Lotus-Eaters in Sicily, at Acragas or Camarina. Nor were they wanting in Illyria or Scythia or somewhere beyond the Straits of Gibraltar. Nothing in all this has anything to do with the Homeric Lotus-Eaters. Nobody ever knew anything about them not already known to Herodotus; and he knew nothing.

His process of thought is transparent: the Lotus-Eaters of Homer are assumed to be a living nation; Homer says that Odysseus could not weather the southeastern cape of the Peloponnese and was driven by storm-winds for nine days over the sea; where will he land, if not in North Africa? Now by happy chance we have a tale about a tribe on the coast of Tripolitania living on the fruit of a shrub or tree; let us call the shrub 'lotus', and our work is done. True, a wind which prevents you from rounding Cape Malea is not the one to carry you west of Tripoli; true also that the shrub or tree—*Jujúba*, *Zizy-phus*—of which the tribe eats the fruit has nothing what-soever to do with any of the plants called lotus; true, finally, that the result of our researches is disenchanting, for it is not more remarkable that an African tribe should eat these berries than that Greeks should eat olives. There is not, however, time to raise objections. We are quickly diverted to new and much greater marvels[11]—the tale of the Atlantes, who have no dreams; of the land where donkeys never drink; of men whose eyes are in their chests, for they have no heads.

Herodotus is not always to be believed, but he is enchanting; wearisome are most of his followers. Nor are modern speculations more rewarding, though occasionally more risible: have not the Lotus-Eaters lately been made real and relevant, a colony of drop-outs living on drugs, *bhang* possibly, or *hashish*?[12]

Enough of all this pseudo-geography. The Lotus-Eaters of Homer have no home in the real world.[13] They are as fanciful as the Cyclops or Circe. We might say simply, they are figures of folktale; but it is not quite so easy. We have first to ask a question or two.

From Homer's brief story we learnt very little, and were left wondering. What sort of creatures were the Lotus-Eaters? Why did they eat lotus, of all flowers? Did they know what effect their diet would have upon the stranger? Were they perhaps waiting for a victim? They had not in mind (says Odysseus) the killing of his companions; what then did they have in mind? In a folktale, it is very unlikely that the hosts will allow their guests to be taken away, as Odysseus takes them, after they have eaten the magical food. We suspect that these Lotus-Eaters are not ordinary men: creatures of fairyland, perhaps; but whether kindly or malignant? Surely they have a story of their own.

We shall have to look in universal folklore to see if we can identify the tale which Homer has in mind. But, first, there is a curious matter to be perpended. *Lotophagos* means 'eater of lotus'; and it is a fair question to ask, why *lotus*? Of all plants in the world, why has the Homeric story chosen the lotus for the diet of our mild-eyed melancholy friends? Now it happens that there were regions of the world where a flower called 'lotus' was in fact the common food of people; and it is worth-while to consider what those regions were, and what is meant by 'lotus' in this context.

The name 'lotus' was applied by the ancients in-differently to a number of quite different families of plants,[14] notably (1) the true lotus, of which more in a moment; (2) the shrub or tree *Zizyphus, Jujúba*, whose berries were eaten by tribes in North Africa; (3) trefoils, clovers, and melilots. Of these, I leave *Jujúba* and the clovers out of account. The *Jujúba*, which belongs to the family *Rhamnaceae*, owes its inclusion in the list of lotuses solely to the determination of ancient geographers and botanists to find a living tribe which they might identify with the Homeric Lotus-Eaters.[15] The trefoils, clovers, and melilots, which belong to the family *Leguminosae*, have always and rightly been regarded as irrelevant: the spellbinding delicacy of the Lotus-Eaters was certainly not to be identified with this common cattle-fodder.

The lotus which men really ate was what I have called the true lotus, of which there are two varieties to be considered: (1) *Nelumbo*, the Indian lotus, and (2) *Nymphaea*, the Egyptian lotus, both of the family *Nymphaeaceae*.[16]

Begin, O Muse, the tale of *Nelumbo*[17] and *Nymphaea*, from the point where the Sanskrit poems of ancient India leave off.[18] It is necessary to say enough to establish two facts: First, that there were (and are) two kinds of edible lotus, one Indian and one Egyptian; for India and

Egypt are places from which the knowledge of the edible lotus could have been transmitted to Homer through poetry or folklore. Secondly, that the Indian lotus could not have been known to Homer except through continuous tradition from the remote period when the Indo-European peoples had not yet divided into Indians and Europeans.

So first, *Nelumbo*. This is the Indian lotus, a beautiful flower, both holy [19] and useful. 'When Buddha was born, a lotus bloomed where he first touched the ground; he stepped seven steps northward, and a lotus marked each footfall'.[20] Its seeds, which are 'the size of filberts',[21] were,[22] as they still are,[23] a common food. *Nymphaea* is the Egyptian lotus, associated in cult with Isis, Osiris, and Horus.[24] Its seeds are edible; they are small grains, like poppy-seeds. The two plants are alike in being aquatic, with edible seeds; in other respects there is very little resemblance between them. *Nelumbo* is rosy; its leaves are raised high above the water by cylindrical petioles. *Nymphaea* is white or blue; its leaves lie more or less flat on the water. There are differences in the number, shape, and arrangement of the sepals, in the shape and appearance of the petals, in the shape of the leaves, and in the size and structure of the seedpods and their fruits.

Herodotus describes both flowers quite accurately, first *Nymphaea* as follows: 'When the river is full and inundates the plains, many lilies, which the Egyptians call "lotus", grow in the water. They pluck these and dry them in the sun, then they crush the poppy-like centre of the lotus and make loaves of it baked over the fire. The root of this lotus is edible too, and fairly sweet; it is round, about the size of an apple'.[25] So much for *Nymphaea*; now he describes *Nelumbo*: 'There are other lilies, which look like roses, growing in the river too.

The fruit of these grows in a separate calyx growing at the side from the root, shaped very like a wasp's nest.[26] Within this are numerous edible seeds, as big as olive-stones. They are eaten both soft and dried'. The account in Theophrastus[27] is similar, but with much additional detail, keenly observed and accurately described. Modern descriptions of *Nelumbo* and *Nymphaea* correct the ancient in a few details only; they add that *Nelumbo* has been a common food in our own times.

Now it is as certain as such things can be that the Indian lotus, *Nelumbo*, well-known to Herodotus, was in his day a recent immigrant from the East. It was not familiar to the Egyptians till the later years of the sixth century B.C.[28] The eating of *Nelumbo* could not have been known to Homer, unless the knowledge had been transmitted through saga or folklore from the remote 'Indo-European' period, a couple of thousand years before the *Odyssey*.

There is much more that might be said about *Nelumbo* and *Nymphaea*; but we already have what we need. We asked, why eaters of lotus, of all flowers in the world? And we have found that the lotus is a flower of which the seeds were in fact a common food, in India and in Egypt. Homer's tale is plainly fiction; but it is fiction blended with dimly remembered fact.

I call it dimly remembered, because the lotus would not have been chosen by Homer if its true nature had not been forgotten. What Homer needed was a mysterious flower with fruits of magical quality; but the flower of which he tells was one of the commonest, in India and in Egypt, and its fruits were the normal food of the masses. This truth must have been long forgotten by Homer's time. In the Dark Age of Greece, from the fall of the Mycenaean kings down to the eighth century

B.C., nothing whatsoever was known about India except the little that had survived in saga and folklore from the very remote past. Nor was anything known about Egypt, except scraps of information (and not many of them) preserved from the Mycenaean period mainly in the tradition of epic verse. But there will have been, at some early period, a traveller's tale of remote regions of the world full of great wonders, such as a tribe of men who lived on flowers which they called 'lotus'. After the lapse of hundreds of years, all contact with reality is lost. Nothing is remembered except that there was an old story about people called 'lotus-eaters'. They were once a traveller's tale, and a true one. Now they no longer have a home in the real world; and we no longer know (or care) what sort of flower this 'lotus' is. If it be asked whether India or Egypt is likelier to be the source of the tale about eaters of lotus, the best evidence may be the fact (if it is one) that 'lotus' is a word of Semitic origin.[29] If the Homeric lotus reflects the Indian *Nelumbo*—a plant unknown to the Western world until long after Homer's time—I do not understand how the flower could be known to Homer by a Semitic name. So I suppose that Egyptian *Nymphaea* was the diet of the real and remote ancestors of the fictitious Lotus-Eaters of the *Odyssey*. The Mycenaeans traded with Egypt for two or three hundred years; their products are found as far up the Nile as Assouan. Traders returned home with much to tell; and among their tales was this, that people in Egypt lived on a flower which they called 'lotus'.

By Homer's time the Lotus-Eaters have degenerated into figures of folktale. At least that is what they seem to be, in the *Odyssey*. But have they any history as such? The essence of the episode is this: that creatures, whether human or not, living in a remote place, offer food to the traveller; who, if he eats it, loses the desire or the power to return home, and will stay with his hosts forever. Is this a common folktale, like the stories of the Cyclops and Circe?

The answer is that, in one special connexion, it is as common a story as you may find. The special connexion is with the underworld, the abode of the dead. The traveller who visits the underworld may be sure of his return, provided that he refuses food or drink offered by his ghostly entertainers; if he partakes, he must stay there forever.

Thus in the Homeric *Hymn to Demeter*,[30] Persephone has good hope of returning from the underworld to the earth above; but Hades, with a sinister smile and furtive glances round,[31] gave her honeysweet seeds of pomegranate to eat before she left him. She ate them; and not even Zeus could then do more than compromise, granting her eight months of the year on earth and four in the underworld.

Two thousand five hundred years after the *Hymn to Demeter* was composed, this belief has been found to be widespread throughout the world. It is common to the Zulus, the Maoris, the Japanese, the Dakotan Indians, and the Finns. I summarize a few examples:

(1) A tale from New Zealand.[32] Mr. Shortland's servant Te Wharewera told the following story about an aunt of his. She died, and her body was left in her hut, and the doors and windows were made fast. A day or two later, Te Wharewera, paddling his canoe on the river in the early morning, was greatly surprised to see his aunt beckoning to him from the bank. She had come to life again, evidently; but she was weak and cold and very hungry. She had a strange tale to tell. Surviving

perilous and eerie adventures on her way to the under-world, she had reached a place where the ghosts of her family were assembled. 'They saluted her, and welcomed her with the wailing chant which Maoris always address to people met after long absence'. Now suddenly the ghost of her father asked whether anyone was left on earth to take care of her child, his grandson. There was not: and her father ordered her at once to return to earth and take care of the child. This she could still do, because she had not yet eaten the food offered her by the ghosts. They tried to compel her to eat, but her father got her safely away. If she had eaten the ghostly food, she would have had to stay there forever. Now she is safely on earth again; but she is very hungry.

(2) A tale told to David Leslie by a Zulu,[33] rendered as closely as possible to the Zulu's words: 'My brother died and was "flung away" in the usual manner. We dug a hole and sat him up in it, put in his blanket, his dress, his sticks, assegais and mat, beside him, covered him up, and left him. Next day we saw him walking up to the kraal . . . He told us that he had been in a fine country, where the corn and sugar-cane grew thick and tall, and the cattle were as fat as fat could be; and that he had met a cousin of his who had died a long time before, who told him to go back immediately, that instant, "because", said he, "you will meet someone else just now if you don't, who will give you food, and then you must remain an *Ehlose* [a sort of ghost; 'familiar spirit'] for ever". . . . I said, "wow!" and came home, thinking, ah! what a delightful country I have been in!' 'Then why didn't he stay there?' I asked. 'He couldn't, you know, after the *Ehlose* of one of his relatives had told him to go back'. 'And suppose he had met the *Ehlose* of a stranger, what would have been the consequence?' . . .

'He would have given him food, he would have taken it, and he would then have been obliged to remain'. This is part of a long story, with a happy ending.

(3) Another tale from the Maoris of New Zealand.[34] There was a beautiful woman named Pare, living in a fine house. 'She had everything to make it nice, beautiful mats, parawais, kaitakas, and topunis, with every kind of perfume, even to that of the kawa kawa'. She fell in love with a great chief named Hutu. Hutu was a married man; with firm but untimely virtue he repulsed her vigorous advances; and she killed herself. Hutu accepted blame for her death and went to rescue her spirit from the underworld. A weird female named Hine nui te po 'cooked food for him, beat the fern-root and put it into a basket, saying, "When you reach the lower regions, eat sparingly of your provisions that they may last, and you may not be compelled to partake of their food, for if you do, you cannot return upwards again"'.

The sequel of this story is irrelevant but very exciting. In brief, Hutu rescued the spirit of Pare, returned to her house, and united her spirit with her body, which had been left there unburied. She was thus fully restored to life; and her tribe was grateful to Hutu. They implored him to marry Pare. Hutu answered, 'But what shall I do with my wife and children?' They replied, '*me puna rua*, take two wives'. Hutu had not thought of that. 'He consented, and they called Pare, "Pare Hutu"'.

(4) A tale from Japan.[35] Izanagi and Izanami are the primary god and goddess in Japanese mythology. They procreated the various islands of Japan and the deities of trees, herbs, sun, moon, earth, water, wind, food, and fire. In giving birth to the last of these, the fire-god, Izanami died. She went down to the land of Yomi, or Hades. Izanagi went to rescue her, but 'he was too late

to bring her back, as she had already eaten of the cooking-furnaces of Yomi'. The story is long, with a most unhappy ending.

(5) A tale from Melanesia.[36] A woman descended to the realm of the ghosts because 'she much desired to see her lately dead brother'. She found him 'lying in a house, because as a recent ghost he was not strong enough to move about'. 'He cautioned her to eat nothing there, and she returned'.

The essence of this very widespread story is that a person, whether living or dead, cannot enter the world of the dead unless he first eats their food, and cannot return from that world if he does eat it. Now there is not the faintest indication in the *Odyssey* that Odysseus has arrived at the threshold of the underworld, or that the Lotus-Eaters are ghosts or demons beyond the grave.[37] Let us therefore briefly consider something else which they might be; for this motif, though specially common in connexion with visits to the world of the dead, is not wholly restricted to that connexion. It is applied (in various forms) also to the world of fairies, goblins, gnomes, giants, and other such daydream and nightmare figures of folklore. A few examples will serve:

(a) A tale from the Isle of Man.[38] 'A man attracted one night, as he was crossing the mountains, by fairy music, entered a fairy hall where a banquet was going on. He noticed among them several faces which he seemed to know, but no act of mutual recognition took place till he had some drink offered him, when one of those whom he seemed to know warned him not to taste of the drink if he had any wish to make his way home again'.

(b) A tale from the Deccan.[39] After many adventures

the hero, a young prince, married Panch-Phul-Ranee, 'the five-flower queen', so called because she weighed no more than five white lotus-flowers. The prince and his young wife and baby were starving in the forest. The prince went to a village for food; but the village was full of conjurors, dancers, and drummers, who thought what a handsome drummer the prince would make. So when he asked for food, they gave him something specially prepared. And as soon as he had eaten it, 'he forgot about his wife and little child, his journey, and all that had ever happened to him in his life before'. He stayed with the conjurors as chief drummer for eighteen years.

(c) A tale from the Faroe Islands about demons who live in lonely hills, the *Huldervolk*, or Hidden People.[40] 'The young females of the Hidden People often fall in love with young men and so try to seduce them and attract them. When the boys go out into the waste-land and become thirsty and tired, the hill opens and a maiden emerges to offer them a drink, beer or milk. If they do not blow the froth off the top, they lose their memory as they drink, for the magic lies in the froth. So the girls bewitch the boys, get power over them, and take them off into the goblins' hill'.

Other examples may be found among the adventures of Wäinamöinen in the Finnish epic *Kalevala*[41] and in the tale of Gormo, Thorkill, and Guthmund in the *Danish History* of Saxo Grammaticus.[42] Common to these and many other tales[43] is the same motif that we found in the underworld stories: the traveller, if he eats what is offered, whether by gentle fairy or by malignant goblin or giant, must stay forever; and very often he forgets the past.

So the Lotus-Eaters might be either ghosts in the underworld or goblins in fairyland; and it is characteristic of our poet that he should portray them as neither the one thing nor the other. Homer takes the motif from folktale and transplants it into a quite different soil. He is, as usual, at pains to suppress, or at least to minimize, the unreal elements in the folktales from which he freely borrows. He makes the scene lifelike and credible. His travellers are ordinary persons on their way home, driven by storm-winds to a distant but not supernatural place; they are not visitors to the underworld or adventurers on the border of fairyland. And the Lotus-Eaters seem quite normal people, except for their peculiar diet. They seem unaware of the effect which their food will have on the strangers. They mean no great harm (we are told); and certainly no great harm is done. Odysseus can take his companions away, none the worse; and the Lotus-Eaters offer no resistance. This characteristic of Homeric art, the adaptation of common folktale motifs to realistic settings, is to be observed throughout the *Odyssey*; especially in the story of the return from Troy to Ithaca, but also elsewhere.[44]

So much for this episode. We have lived an hour with the Lotus-Eaters and learnt a little of their history. They have their origin in a true but dimly remembered tale about men in Egypt who lived on lotus. Now to their lotus the poet ascribes a certain magical effect which he takes from common folklore. But the magic is hardly done before it is undone. We—the audience of Homer— are in a real world, and we believe every word we are told.

I have hardly concealed the fact that I am fond of the Lotus-Eaters. I leave them now, reluctantly, in their

Tennysonian home, mild-eyed and melancholy, 'propt on beds of amaranth and moly', among their 'wavering light and shadows', 'eating the Lotos day by day', and playing sweet music that 'softer falls than petals from blown roses on the grass'.

II

The
Laestrygonians

II

Odyssey 10.80–132: 'Six days we sailed on, night and day alike. And on the seventh we came to the citadel of Lamos, strong-gated Laestrygonia, where the shepherd driving home calls to the shepherd driving out, and he can hear him. In that place a man who never slept could have carried off a double wage, the one for tending cattle, the other for pasturing white sheep; for the paths of Night and Day are close together. There, when we came to a fine harbor, round which a sheer rock-cliff was set continuously on both sides, and projecting beaches reach forward opposite each other in the harbor-mouth, and narrow is the entrance—there they all held their curved ships inside. So these were moored inside the hollow harbor, one beside another; for no wave ever swelled in it, neither great nor small, but there was a bright calm all round it. But I alone stayed my black ship outside, just there on the edge, fastening the cables from a rock. And I went up to a rugged look-out, and stood there. In that place neither works of oxen nor of men appeared; smoke alone we see springing from the ground. Thereupon I sent companions to go and learn what the men might be who ate bread in the land; I chose two men, and as third I gave a herald to go with them. These disembarked and walked a smooth road, where wagons used to bring down timber to the city from the high hills. And they met a maiden drawing water in front of the city, the noble daughter of the Laestrygon Antiphates. She had gone down to the fair-flowing spring Artacia, for that is where they used to carry water to the city from. And they stood beside her and spoke to her, and asked who might be the king of this people, and what men he ruled. She at once showed them her father's high-roofed dwelling. And when they entered the fine dwelling, they found that woman, his wife, as tall as a mountain peak; and they detested her. Quickly from the meeting-place she called great Antiphates, her husband, who devised a pitiable doom for them. At once he seized one of my companions, and prepared to eat him. The other two darted off in flight and reached the ships. But the king made hue and cry throughout the city, and the noble Laestrygonians heard him and came from all quarters, in thousands, resembling giants, not men. They pelted them from the cliffs with boulders big as a man could carry, and throughout the ships there rose an evil clangour of men dying and ships splintering all at once. They speared our men like fishes, and carried their dismal dinner home. While they were killing them inside the deep harbour, I drew my sharp sword from my thigh, and with it I cut away the cables from my dark-prowed ship, and at once I exhorted and commanded my companions to fall upon the oars, that we might escape disaster. And all of them flung the sea-water high, in fear of death; and gladly my ship escaped seaward from the overhanging cliffs. But all the other ships were lost then and there'.

The Laestrygonians, like the Lotus-Eaters, have been sadly neglected. The Homeric story is indeed wonderfully illustrated in a work of art, found at Rome in 1840, of the first century B.C.; one of the best landscape paintings that have survived from antiquity.[1] There is no other representation in art, and references in the poetical and romantic writers of Greece and Rome are very few. In Greek, I notice only the insufferable Lycophron, a brief mention of γῆν ἔσπερον Λαιστρυγόνων.[2] In Latin, Ovid once[3] re-tells Homer's tale in ten lines, and in another place briefly refers to it.[4] Juvenal mentions them contemptuously, *inmanis Laestrygonas atque Cyclo-pas*.[5] In Horace, Statius, and Silius Italicus the Laestrygonians' name occurs half a dozen times as a geographical term[6]; and it is their geographical location only that interests other writers. Speculation had been rife long before Thucydides. Describing Sicily, he says, 'Of a certain part of the country, the oldest inhabitants are said to have been the Cyclopes and the Laestrygonians. I personally have no idea what race they were or where they came from or where they went. You must be content with what the poets have said and the opinions of individuals about these matters'.[7]

It is probable that the Laestrygonians, like the Lotus-Eaters, were known to posterity only from the story in the *Odyssey*. It seemed necessary to find a home for them; and it is remarkable that one should have been found already in the time of Hesiod: they lived (he seems to say) in Sicily, near Mount Etna.[8] The world accepted this for a long time, defining the place more specifically as the town of Leontini.[9] But it was not the whole truth: the day came when someone found reason to assert that Leontini was not their original home; they were immigrants from Italy, specifically from the region around Formiae and Caieta in Campania.[10]

Let us put all this harmless nonsense gently aside and look at something of interest.

Only eighty lines (say, ten minutes' recitation time) separate the story of the Laestrygonians from the story of the Cyclops; yet the two stories have much in common. Both the Cyclops and the Laestrygonians are giants; both are cannibals; both pursue the hero and attack his ships from the cliff-top with large rocks. The principal persons and, in outline, the events seem much alike in both stories, and we were not expecting, having heard the story of the Cyclops at great length, now almost immediately to hear the similar story of the Laestrygonians.

I shall return to this point. At present I focus attention not on similarity but on differences.

Tales about ogres are very common in folklore. The type represented by the Cyclops is widespread throughout the world.[11] The essence of that story is the blinding of a one-eyed cannibal giant by the hero, who may be assisted by companions. The type represented by the Laestrygonian story is not so common, but still widespread. It has no one-eyed ogre and no blinding; and it has a quite different beginning. It regularly starts with the hero entering the ogre's home and finding there only the ogre's womenfolk; usually his wife, occasionally mother or daughters. The following action is therefore very different from that of the Cyclops version: it consists of the hero's dealings with the womenfolk, and the story is usually near its end before the ogre appears, called home as a rule by his wife; and so it happens in the *Odyssey*. Only the end is much the same in both versions—pursuit by the ogre, and the hero's escape.

The Laestrygonian version is found (with much variation in the detail) in the folktales of peoples as far apart as the natives of New Zealand, Zululand, Tibet, and North America.[12] Similarity to the Homeric story, and difference from it, are well illustrated by an example taken from the selection published by Leo Frobenius,[13] a folktale from Heiltsuk:

'Four brothers, setting out to hunt, are warned not to enter a house from which reddish smoke ascends. In this house lives the cannibal-ogre, whose name means, in English, "he who first ate human flesh at the point where the river enters the sea". Despite the warning they enter the house. They find a woman and her child at home.' The child manifests a lively desire to eat the visitors, who would prefer, but are not free, to be elsewhere. The eldest brother devises an ingenious plan for their escape: 'He shoots an arrow into the distance, for one of the others to go and fetch. He shoots off three arrows, and so three brothers get away. To the woman's questions he explains that his brothers will soon be back (they have gone to fetch the arrows). But then he shoots off another arrow, and goes to fetch it, and so he too escapes. Now the woman shouts to her husband, "Come home. I have let an excellent dinner get away". The ogre comes home, and sets out in pursuit of the brothers. The eldest brother throws a whetstone, a comb, and fish-oil behind him as he runs, and these turn into a mountain, a jungle, and an ocean. When the ogre nevertheless penetrates to the brothers' house, he falls into a moat and is killed by red-hot stones heaped upon him'.

The *Odyssey* has all the essence of this and some of its detail; for instance, the distant view of smoke rising from the ogre's home, and the woman's call to the ogre. But it differs, as usual, in the realism of its setting. Homer's Laestrygonian is gigantic in stature but otherwise human and indeed partly hellenized. He is king of a nation; has a good Greek name; lives in a high-roofed palace; and is presently to be found in the *agora*, the place of meeting and marketing. The magical elements in the tale of pursuit and escape are eliminated; they are replaced by a realistic action which assists the progress of the main theme of Odysseus' return to Ithaca. The whole is credible, except that the Laestrygonians are giants; and we, the audience of Homer in the eighth century B.C., are by no means certain that they were not. They

ROCKINGHAM PUBLIC LIBRARY
HARRISONBURG, VIRGINIA 22801

'command, if not exactly belief, at least imaginative assent'.[14]

The realism of the story is enhanced by the manner of its telling. So long as normal events are to be described, the narrative is leisurely and full. You will have noticed that there was much detail about the harbor; about the mooring of the ships; about sending a mission inland. Even the path of the mission from the fleet was described with customary Homeric fulness: it was 'a smooth road, by which the wagons used to bring down timber from the high hills to the city'. And there was time to stop for a word with a girl drawing water in the suburbs, like Rebecca in Genesis, who 'came forth with her pitcher on her shoulder, and she went down to the well, and drew water'; this girl (by the way), who shows the hero the path to the house, is a common and characteristic figure of folktales.[15] But now, when you actually meet the supernatural villains, the giants who can (as it were) eat you while you wait, the tempo of the narrative changes suddenly. From this moment onwards it is a gallop to the goal. There are only twenty lines for the whole adventure—the interview with the queen, her summoning of the king, his killing and cooking an ambassador, the flight of the others, the hue and cry, the chase, the bombardment of the ships by the giants, their harpooning of the men, the escape of Odysseus. You are given no time to reflect that you are, for a moment, out of contact with the real world.

As for the queen, no grimmer female was ever more briefly described. She is unforgettable: but all that is said about her is that she was as tall as a mountain, and they detested her. When we met her daughter at the well in the suburbs, we found in her a certain charm. Nothing was said about her being out-size and overweight, and we could not have guessed that she had a mother like this. Her father, King Antiphates, is brisk enough: within ten words of his summons from the market-place he is cooking an ambassador. His compatriots need only three words to fish their victims from the sea, and three more to take them home and eat them. The contrast between this passage and the leisurely narratives which precede and follow is obvious and was surely intentional. The unreal elements in the story are to be hurried over; and we notice that the rocks which the giants throw at the ships, though large, are not so very far from the normal. They are ἀνδραχθέα; a man could carry them, though he could not throw them.

I now return to an earlier point. I observed that, despite the differences, there are obvious similarities between the story of the Cyclops and the story of the Laestrygonians. They are both variations on the theme of the cannibal giant. And, having just heard the story of the Cyclops at great length, we were not expecting to hear another variation on the same theme very soon afterwards. Let us reflect upon this matter.

First, it is plain that the story of the Laestrygonians is not merely brief; it is also abbreviated. It implies a long story, here reduced to an elliptic and allusive summary. The entire episode, starting from the introduction of the ogre's daughter, is told in about a hundred and fifty words, less than two minutes' recitation time. It will be generally agreed that this is a synopsis of a story told on other occasions at much greater length. But why then is such a synopsis included almost immediately after the similar story of the Cyclops?

The most obvious explanation would presuppose that the story of the Cyclops and (in its longer version) the story of the Laestrygonians were both popular recitations in the epic about Odysseus. You might hear the one or the other, but you would not expect to hear both from the same poet on the same occasion, for the tales are too much alike. But when the old recitations about Odysseus were combined into a continuous epic, the poet makes a choice. He chooses the Cyclops, and tells that story at great length; but also, to the great satisfaction of his audience, he adds a brief sketch of the similar story which they know so well, the Laestrygonian adventure. Nothing but the radical change of technique —the synoptic treatment and the breathless hurry of it—saves it from falling rather flat; it moves too fast to fall down.

But there might be a quite different explanation. The story of the Cyclops is a universal folktale, adopted by the Odyssean saga, which substituted the person of Odysseus for the hero of the folktale (in which he is very often nameless). Now the Laestrygonians also are figures of a common folktale, and we have to consider the possibility that this is the first time that anybody has ever heard Odysseus identified with its hero. In that case the poet would be entertaining his audience with an innovation, springing a surprise on them by giving them this lively sketch of a folktale which they have heard very often, though they have never before heard it adapted to the adventures of Odysseus.

Our choice between these alternative explanations will be affected by the answer to another question: is there any indication that the Laestrygonian adventures had long been the subject of oral epic poetry? If it was merely an old folktale, not versified, not adopted by the professional singers, its hero might be anybody, variable from place to place; the poet might include it here as a novelty, an episode which had never before been associated with this or any other saga. But if it had long been embodied in the traditional oral epic, it is certain that its hero will have been identified already with a person familiar to Greek legend.

I believe that there is at least one definite indication that the Laestrygonian adventure had long been included in the traditional epic repertoire, though the hero associated with the adventure was not, at least in one earlier version, Odysseus.

Consider first the words in verses 81–82: 'We came to the steep citadel of Lamos, *Τηλέπυλον Λαιστρυγονίην*'. Now ask, first, is 'Lamos' a proper name or a place name? Homeric usage is no sure guide; in the old epic, the genitive name may be a man, as in *Πριάμου πόλις*, or a place, as in *'Ιλίου . . . πτολίεθρον*. We soon discover that the king of Laestrygonia is named Antiphates; and you might infer that the poet must have taken Lamos to be a place name. For if 'Lamos' is a person, and you speak of 'the city of Lamos', must he not be king of the place named after him? And how then shall we account for the fact that the king is called not Lamos but Antiphates? The inference is insecure, for a city may be called by the name of an earlier king: Pylos is called *Νηλήιος* long after the death of Neleus, and Cos is called 'the city of Eurypylus', after the name of its founder, not its present king. We must look elsewhere for an answer; and surely we find one in the words *Τηλέπυλον Λαιστρυγονίην*. Postpone for a moment the question which of these two words is the place name; whichever you choose, neither is compatible with 'Lamos' as a place name. Consider first the rendering 'Laestrygonia, the citadel of the place Lamos': This implies a territory called Lamos, with a fortress inside it called

Laestrygonia. I am quite sure that the poet did not mean this. Laestrygonia is the regional or national name. These people are Laestrygonians, not Lamians, and 'Laestrygonia' is not merely the name of the citadel in a country called 'Lamos'. Now take 'Telepylus' as a place name: 'Laestrygonian Telepylus, the citadel of the place Lamos'. The objection is the same in principle: these people are Laestrygonians, not Lamians; their royal citadel might have some special name, 'Telepylus', but it will be the citadel of a people called Laestrygonians, not of a country called Lamos inhabited by a people called (for no imaginable reason, in that case) 'Laestrygonians'.

But now, is 'Telepylus' in fact a place name or an adjective? Is it 'far-gated Laestrygonia' or 'Laestrygonian Telepylus'? Is there any means of deciding? For some reason, if any, not known to me, most modern editors and other writers generally agree, and agree in what I take to be the opposite of the truth. They print capital 'T', $T\eta\lambda\acute{\epsilon}\pi\upsilon\lambda o\nu$, as if there were, or could be, a city name 'Telepylus'; and you may think that nobody could positively refute them. I believe that the choice is not so free, indeed not free at all.

For how many city names in Greek lands are known to us; and how many of them are compounds with the suffix from $\pi\acute{\upsilon}\lambda\eta$, 'a gate'? I do not know how to settle this question except by looking at each name in one of the larger atlas-indexes. Take one which contains about nine thousand entries, and you will not find a single example. There was not one city name in the history of Greece with a suffix from $\pi\acute{\upsilon}\lambda\eta$. There are three or four uncompounded 'Pylae', in the plural, of mountain passes or the like, not of cities; and the only compound of the plural 'Pylae' is Thermopylae, the name of a landscape, not a city. 'Telepylus' would be unique in Greek nomenclature. It has the sheepish look of the exposed impostor. Never in history, never in legend, did the Greeks make a compound city name of which the second element was -πυλος, 'gated'.

And why should we? The alternative, to take it as an adjective, is very easy. For although compound adjectives with the suffix -πυλος are not common, we are familiar with 'seven-gated Boeotian Thebes', ἑπτάπυλος; 'hundred-gated Egyptian Thebes', ἑκατόμπυλος; 'high-gated Troy', ὑψίπυλος. It is as good as certain that τηλέπυλος is an epithet, not a place name. So 'Laestrygonia' must be the place name here, and Lamos will then be a person, not a place. We can now confidently translate the text, 'The steep citadel of [a person named] Lamos, something-gated Laestrygonia'.

'*What*-gated'? What does τηλέπυλος mean? Certainly not 'With gates *far apart*', the rendering in Liddell and Scott (who add that 'it is now written Telepylus, as a proper-name'); τηλέπυλος could not possibly mean that. The Dindorfs' lexicon offers an alternative, 'Whose gates are a long way off'. Ancient scholars were as uneasy as the modern: the Homeric scholia[16] say that some took the word to be a place name, others an adjective; and that some understood 'Whose gates are far apart *from each other*', implying a very large city, others 'Whose gates have each one side far apart from the other side', implying very broad gates.

This is all obviously rubbish; let us sweep it from the surface of the word. Τηλέπυλος could not possibly mean or imply 'having gates at a great distance *from each other*', let alone 'having a gate of which one side is a long way from the other side'. If τηλε- has anything to do with distance, τηλέπυλος could only mean 'far-gated', and that could imply nothing but 'having its gates a long way off'. I have no hesitation in rejecting that as spurious coinage. All cities have their gates a long way off, if you happen to be a long way from them; and why specify the *gates*? Nobody in the world ever coined an epithet to inform you that a city has its *gates* a long way off; and you will not be surprised to hear that the Greek language has no other τηλε- compound of which the second half refers to a physical object. The second half of τηλε- compounds is always verbal, in effect if not in form; and this is natural, not accidental. There is a use for adjectives composed of 'far' plus a verb, such as 'far-seeing', 'far-shooting', 'far-famed', 'far-travelling'; the world has never had a use for adjectives composed of 'far' plus a noun, such as 'far-tabled', 'far-horsed', 'far-hatted', or 'far-gated'.

Ruthless reasoning has led us to a prospect which we contemplate with our customary stoical calm. Since τηλέπυλος would be rubbish if τηλε- signified 'distance', we infer that τηλε- does not signify 'distance'. And our lively minds leap to another Odyssean compound of τηλε- with a nonverbal suffix, in which τηλε- cannot possibly mean 'far'. The son of Odysseus is Τηλέμαχος, plainly a Greek word, and -μαχος means 'fighter'; but what does Τηλε- mean? Certainly not 'at a distance'. The Homeric hero is the opposite, ἀγχίμαχος, ἀγχιμαχητής, one who fights hand to hand. Name your son 'fighter at a distance', and you christen him a coward, or at best an eccentric irregular like the Locrians, who keep away from pitched battles, fighting from a distance with unheroic bow and arrow, despised by the regular army. Plainly Τηλέμαχος must have meant something of good omen, for example 'strong fighter', 'good fighter', a companion for Ἀλκίμαχος, Καλλίμαχος, and the like.

It seems certain that τηλε- in *Τηλέμαχος* and *τηλέπυ-λος* represents some obsolete adjective of quality, 'good, fine, strong', or the like; we cannot hope, on this evidence, to define its content more closely. There may be a few other examples: *Τηλε-* in the name *Τηλεδίκη* certainly, and in the name *Τηλέγονος* probably, has nothing to do with 'distance'.

Certainly, too, τηλ- in *τηλύγετος* has nothing to do with 'distance'. Whether *τηλ-* in this word is the same as *τηλ-* in *τηλέπυλος*, we cannot tell. *Τηλύγετος*, like *τηλέπυλος*, is an obsolete relic of older Greek. If *τηλ(-)* meant much the same thing as *καλλι-*, nothing would remain unexplained; there would be no mystery about *Καλλίμαχος*, *Καλλιδίκη*, *καλλίπυλος*.

The form of the adjective raises a question. If the first component is adjectival, it cannot end in -ε; I suppose that original *τηλι-* or *τηλο-* or *τηλυ-* was replaced in the course of time by *τηλε-* under the influence of the common *τηλε-* ('distance') compounds.

The important fact about the adjective *τηλέπυλος* (whatever its proper form and whatever its precise meaning) is that it contains an element, *τηλε-*, which was plainly obsolete already in Homer's time. The compound as a whole, *τηλέπυλος*, occurs nowhere else, either in Homer or later; and the element *τηλε-*, in the sense in which it is used in *Τηλέμαχος* and *τηλέπυλος*, has no future at all. Such obsolete words were preserved only because they were embedded in traditional epic formulas; they must be very old, among the oldest elements in the Homeric poems. The poet has this adjective here simply because it is and always has been fixed in this part of the verse, inseparably linked to the noun *Λαιστρυγονίη*; neither he nor anyone else knew what it meant. The tale of the Laestrygonians, abbreviated in the *Odyssey*, must have had a long history in verse before Homer.

This inference is strengthened by the fact that τηλέπυλος occurs here in association with two names, Λάμος and Λαιστρυγονία, of which the former probably and the latter certainly is not Greek. Λαιστρυγονία occurs nowhere else; it is plainly a barbarian name. Λάμος occurs almost nowhere except (very rarely) as a river name. The Greek epic does not invent barbarian names; generally it hellenizes such barbarian names as it must use; and if it needs to invent a name for a barbarian, it makes a Greek one. It is likely that the folktale about Lamos and Laestrygonia came to the Greeks from the pre-Greek population. It was versified, and the formula Λάμοι᾽ αἰπὺ πτολίεθρον, τηλέπυλον Λαιστρυγονίην, came down to the *Odyssey* from a remote era in which the component τηλε- was still alive and creative, indeed a suitable element for the hero's son's name, Τηλέμαχος.

We began with the question whether the Laestrygonian adventure was embedded in the oral epic tradition or is merely a recently versified folktale; and our question is now answered by the observation that the phrasing in Homer's verse bears the hallmark of great antiquity. And then we asked another question: if the Laestrygonian adventure was part of the traditional epic repertoire, the poets will almost certainly have identified the hero with some person familiar in Greek legend; was that person Odysseus, or is the poet at least to this extent springing a surprise on his audience? Is he transferring this tale from some other person to Odysseus? There is a single clue to the answer, the name of the fountain 'Artacia' in verse 108.

There was only one fountain 'Artacia' in the ancient

world; it was (and still is—'Artaki') at Cyzicus in the
Propontis; and its great fame was its association with an
ancient legend, the story of Jason and the Argonauts. It
is well known that the *Odyssey* has transferred to
Odysseus a number of adventures which had hitherto
belonged to Jason,[17] and this is presumably one of them.
Circe and the Wandering Rocks, possibly the Sirens and
the Cattle of the Sun too, belong properly to the story
of Jason and the Argonauts; the *Odyssey* uprooted them
and replanted them, not at all deeply, in its own tale.
'Artacia' comes from the same source; and we now see
the Laestrygonians in a new light. At first this episode
looked like an imitation, in miniature, of the story of the
Cyclops. Now it looks quite different—a synopsis of a tale
well known from the Argonautic saga, here for the first
time transferred to Odysseus. Ἀργὼ πᾶσι μέλουσα,[18]
said our poet, 'the vessel Argo is in all your minds; you
know the story, but this is the first time you have heard
it with Odysseus for hero instead of Jason'.

Finally, a word about the much-debated lines 82–86:[19]

> ... Laestrygonia, where the shepherd driving home calls
> to the shepherd driving out, and he hears him. In that place
> a man who never slept could have carried off a double wage,
> the one for tending cattle, the other for pasturing white
> sheep; for the paths of Night and Day are near.

The general sense of lines 82–85 is clear. Herdsmen go
out at daybreak and come in at nightfall. So when you
say that the herdsman going to work meets the herdsman returning from work, and that the man who could
go without sleep could do a double shift and earn a
double wage, you imply that daylight prevails for

almost the whole twenty-four hours. And when you
explain this by adding that the paths of Night and Day
are 'near', you must mean 'near to each other'. Night
and Day are supernatural beings who move across the
sky. In normal conditions their paths will follow the
same lines across the sky, and the one does not begin
until the other is finished; the movements of Night and
Day are thus as far apart as they can be in the circumstances. But in the land of the Laestrygonians conditions
are not normal. The time of Night is very short, and the
normal relation between the paths of Night and Day is
therefore quite altered. In that peculiar region, at the
edge of the world, where Day prevails almost the whole
of the twenty-four hours, Night is closely surrounded by
Day. Night has indeed almost no path at all, and the
little it has is pressed upon and almost encroached upon
by Day's path, both in space and in time.[20]

We do not know exactly how Homer envisaged the
motions of Night and Day either in normal or in these
abnormal circumstances. Briefly, the Greek epic supposes the surface of the earth to be a more or less flat
disc; the sky is an inverted bowl covering the disc; round
the edges of the disc flows a circular river called *Okeanos*;
the disc—the surface of the earth—is the top of a cylinder
which extends downwards as far as the sky extends upwards. The sun rises from the river *Okeanos* in the east
and sets in the river *Okeanos* in the west.[21] We do not
know how the sun got back to its starting point in the
east; nor do we know where Night had its starting point
or how it returned to it. It is a fair guess that the account
given by Hesiod in the *Theogony* (lines 746ff.) reflects the
prevailing opinion on these matters: Atlas holds up the
sky, 'at the point where Night and Day, going close
together,[22] speak to each other as they cross the great

bronze threshold'. Hesiod is describing normal conditions. He is thinking of nights and days of normal length, and his description implies that, whereas Day travels from east to west, Night spreads over the sky from the west; for otherwise Night and Day could not 'cross the threshold' at the same moment. Night departs, and enters the sky, as Day arrives, at the end of its journey, in the west; and they have a moment for conversation at the doorway. We are left wondering how Day gets back to the east, and Night back to the west. Night may well be supposed to recede at daybreak back to its home in the west, driven back by the advancing light from the east; but the manner of Day's return from west to east is not known. Before very long, in the poems of Mimnermus and Stesichorus,[23] we shall hear of the golden bowl which carries the sun and its horses and chariot back from west to east during the night, sailing on the river *Okeanos* round the edge of the earth; but there is no mention of this in Homer or Hesiod.

A peculiar feature of these lines is the apparent knowledge, unexpected at this time and in this part of the world, that there is a region of the earth in which the nights may be very short. Eight or nine hundred years later Tacitus will tell the astonished Romans that 'in the most distant region of Britain the night is so short that the end and beginning of daylight are separated only by the finest of distinctions';[24] but how could the prehistoric Greeks have known about such phenomena in the remote north?

In reality, where short nights occur, they will be balanced by long nights: was Homer aware of this too?

In that place are the city and people of the Kimmerians, who are cloaked in mist and cloud, and the blazing Sun never looks down upon them with its rays, neither when it rises to the starry sky nor when it turns again from earth to the sky, but deadly night is stretched over miserable mortals. (*Odyssey* 11.14ff.)

Ancient readers supposed, and most modern readers agree, that this passage reveals knowledge of the long winter nights of the north;[25] but I think it likelier that the picture drawn here is wholly mythical. Homer is speaking of perpetual night, not of abnormally long nights. Odysseus has reached the edge of the earth; the scene is close to the threshold of Hades, and it is not surprising that total darkness should prevail there. The Kimmerians are indeed a real people, but Homer knows nothing about them except their name and the fact that they live on the verge of the earth in the northeast; fiction or fable supplies the perpetual night which is said to envelop them.

Now what might be Homer's source for the notion that there is a region of the earth where the days are extremely long and the nights extremely short?[26]

Let us first consider whether the origin may lie in myth or folktale, having no relation to the real world. Thus, for example, the virtuous in the afterworld enjoy perpetual sunlight, according to Pindar:

$$\text{τοῖσι μὲν λάμπει σθένος ἀελίου}$$
$$\text{τὰν ἐνθάδε νύκτα κάτω,}$$

fr. 129

'For them the sun shines strong below, while here it is night'. But this example exposes the weakness of the explanation: it is natural to think of Heaven as a place of perpetual sunlight, of Hell as a place of perpetual darkness; but Homer is talking of something very different—of a peculiar relation between day and night, such that there is indeed a night, but it is a very short one. I may add also that he is talking not about Heaven or any other region of bliss, but about a land of cannibal ogres.

A quite different explanation was offered in antiquity. Crates, first head of the great library at Pergamon in the second century B.C., wrote on this passage of the *Odyssey*, and his comment is preserved in effect as follows:

Crates supposes that the nights in Laestrygonia were short; and that the reason for this is that the people lived near the head of the constellation Draco [in the extreme north], about which the astronomer-poet Aratus says 'its head comes down to the point where the limits of setting and rising blend with each other'. Thus, because the star's rising and setting are very close together, Homer can say 'the paths of Night and Day are close'.[27]

This was an ingenious explanation; it may be the truth. A star, such as the head-star of Draco, 'which is so situated that it rises nearly due North, will set nearly due North, and the interval between setting and rising will be very short'.[28] People who live just below the constellation Draco will have a very short star-time, and that means a very short night-time. The Greeks from earliest times had a good general knowledge of the apparent motions of the stars. It was an easy inference that the region immediately below a very short-lived star has a very short night; and this notion may have been familiar in the time of Homer. He needed no amber-trader from the Baltic, no migratory Eskimo or Icelander, to spin him yarns about the midnight sun; though, if one should do so, Homer would believe him without question, for he had guessed as much already.

It may, however, be objected—I am by no means sure that it is true—that Homer has led us to suppose that

Laestrygonia is in the extreme west (originally in the extreme east, if this tale was at home in the Argonautic saga); and the same elementary knowledge of the stars which tells us that the nights are short in the north tells us that they are of normal length in the west or east. Homer is generally vague and inconsistent about geographical and directional detail, but he very seldom talks what the common man would regard as positive nonsense. To transfer short nights from the north to the west would be to contradict the common sense of the shepherd and the sailor—if the notion of short nights was indeed based on observation of the stars.

We may therefore incline, at least provisionally, to consider with sympathy the common opinion: which is that Homer's source is (ultimately) a traveller's tale about the long days and short nights of high northern latitudes.

There is only one likely route by which such a tale might have been transmitted to Mycenaean Greece: by way of the amber-trade from the north coast of Germany.[29] Amber, chemically analysed as Baltic in origin,[30] has been found on a number of Mycenaean sites, notably in some of the shaft-graves at Mycenae and in tholos-tomb 'A' at Kakovatos.[31] Epic poetry preserved the memory of its use as an article of luxury[32] in the remote past (amber was not much used and not much valued in the historical period, until the trade was revived in the late Republic and early Empire at Rome[33]).

It is thus certain that the Mycenaean Greeks were directly or indirectly in contact with traders from the north coast of Germany; but this fact alone is not enough, as all seem to suppose it, for our purpose. For if traders from the Baltic told a tale about their nights and days, it would not have been a tale of almost perpetual daylight or almost perpetual darkness at any season of the year. The most northerly imaginable sources for Mycenaean amber are Jutland and the Kürisches Haff[34] (in the east of Prussia, hard by Lithuania). Now the Kürisches Haff lies below fifty-six degrees north latitude, roughly in the latitude of Glasgow, and the amber-fisheries of Jutland lie mostly about the same latitude. The shortest night of the year in these regions is as long as six and a half hours, and I find it hard to believe that the difference between this and the shortest night at Thebes or Athens would have been a topic worth talking about all the way from the Baltic to the Mediterranean. If the tale about a region of almost perpetual daylight came from the Baltic traders, it must have come to them from others much further north. And it happens that the home of the Baltic amber-fishers is the only one which may have been in contact with the only people living near the Arctic Circle of whom the ancient world could possibly have had any knowledge—the inhabitants of the head of the gulf of Bothnia, only thirty miles from the Arctic Circle. In that region alone of the accessible world there is indeed a period of the year when the duration of the night is measured in minutes; and there might be contact between sea-traders all the way down the gulf of Bothnia to the Kürisches Haff.

You may, however, think it likelier that the notion of almost perpetual daylight is either simply an exaggeration of the difference between the Baltic and Greece, or an inference from it. The Mycenaeans might talk non-sense which happens to be true, as Tacitus talked non-sense which happens to be false. It was really inexcusable for Tacitus to say that in the extreme north of Britain night and day are separable only by the finest of distinctions. Even in the Shetland Isles, two hundred miles north of Scotland, the shortest night is as much as five hours long. The scientific knowledge of Tacitus is indeed below the standard of his time; [35] but he ought to have listened more carefully to his father-in-law Agricola, and he ought to have read Caesar's *Gallic War*. Caesar had heard the story about long winter nights prevailing, not indeed in Britain, but in adjacent islands; and he expresses himself with a caution and precision which should have been a model for Tacitus: 'several smaller islands are supposed to lie close to Britain, about which some have written that in winter the night lasts for thirty continuous days. We could learn nothing about this by inquiry, but by precise water-clock measurements we observed that the nights are shorter than on the continent'. [36]

Tacitus was not the last historian to indulge in this particular exaggeration. The Persian historian of Tamerlane's exploits in the fourteenth century, Sharafeddin Ali, says [37] that his hero 'penetrated to the region of perpetual daylight, a strange phenomenon, which authorized his Mạhometan doctors to dispense with the obligation of evening prayer.' [38] The rays of the setting and of the rising sun, we are told, were hardly separated by any interval. Yet not even the most exaggerated account of Tamerlane's western expeditions ever takes him further north than the sixtieth degree of latitude; and the most reliable leaves him two hundred miles south of Moscow.

When the facts about the relation between night and day in the polar regions had been scientifically ascertained and had become a matter of common knowledge, it was easy for a careless writer to misapply them haphazardly. And the facts had indeed been ascertained hundreds of years before Tacitus. We have had a spherical earth since Pythagoras; we have known the measurement of its circumference since Eratosthenes; earth has rotated about its axis since Heraclides Ponticus; and it has revolved round the sun since Aristarchus the Samian. There was no longer any mystery about the apparent motions of the sun, and it was easy to calculate that the polar regions must have continuous day for six months and continuous night for six months annually. The fact is reported as a commonplace by the elder Pliny.[39] Three hundred years before him, Pytheas of Marseilles[40] visited a land in which, he said, these conditions actually obtained. He called it 'the island of Thule'. If he was telling the truth, he must have reached the coast of Norway about or above the Arctic Circle.

But we are now very far from Homer and the Mycenaeans. They knew nothing about these things. They had no information likely to lead to a theory of almost perpetual daylight, either by way of natural exaggeration or by way of logical inference—unless the theory of Crates is the truth. Wholly perpetual day or night may be invented by priest or poet or fable-teller; but almost perpetual day or night is something different in kind. I have found no likelier explanation of the almost perpetual daylight of Laestrygonia than the transmission of the true fact from the Gulf of Bothnia to the Baltic, from the Baltic down the amber-trail to Greece. If, as I believe, the Laestrygonians were originally at home in the Argonautic legend, Laestrygonia must have been located somewhere in the remote and fabulous northeast, on the shores of the Euxine or Sea of Azov.[41] And it was easy for the epic poet to transfer a motif from the Gulf of Bothnia to the Sea of Azov, so dim and so confused were his notions about the remote northeast. Strabo, the greatest of ancient geographers, is still under the impression, at the beginning of the Christian era, that the Caspian flows into the north German seas.

But now, concerning the Laestrygonians, let so much have been said.

III

Circe

III *Odyssey* 10.133–454: Only one ship escaped from the Laestrygonians. It carried Odysseus and forty-five companions to the island of Aia, where Circe lived. Smoke was seen rising from a house, and Odysseus sent half his company to explore. Led by Eurylochus, they arrived at the palace of Circe in a forest-clearing. And around it were humans transformed into lions and wolves, the victims of Circe's drugs. These did not attack men, but stood up and wagged their long tails, like dogs making friends with their master as he comes from the dinner-table. Circe was sitting indoors and weaving at her loom. The men heard her and called out to her. She opened the door and invited them to enter. All entered except Eurylochus, who guessed that there was some deception. Circe added dismal drugs to a dish of cheese and barley-groats and honey mixed with Pramnian wine. When the men had eaten and drunk, she struck them with her wand, shut them up in her pigsty, and gave them acorns and cornel-cherries to eat. They had the heads and voices and bristles and bodies of pigs, but their minds remained human. Eurylochus returned to Odysseus and told him that his companions had disappeared. They had gone indoors, and none had come out again; he does not know what has happened to them.

Odysseus took his sword and bow and set out alone to look for them. Close to the palace of Circe he met Hermes disguised as a young man, and learnt from him that his companions had been shut up by Circe ὥστε σύες, 'like pigs'. Hermes gave Odysseus a magical plant which the gods call *moly* (we are not told what men call it); it had a black root and milk-white flower, and was difficult for mortals to dig up. This would make it safe for Odysseus to eat the dish of drugs; and when Circe struck him with her wand he must draw his sword and threaten to kill her. She would then invite him to her bed, and he must obey her, because she would then release his companions. But he must exact from her first a great oath; otherwise she might bewitch him when he was defenceless.

All this happened as foretold. Odysseus drank the drugged mixture without harm. Circe struck him with her wand, saying 'Go now to the sty and lie down with the rest of your company'. He attacked her with his sword. She recognized him as Odysseus, and invited him to her bed. He demanded the great oath, and she gave it cheerfully. Next morning four maidservants attended Odysseus. One furnished a throne with purple coverlets and linen cloths; another brought silver tables and golden food-vessels; the third served golden wine-cups from a silver mixing-bowl; the fourth bathed him and clothed him in a fine cloak and tunic. Still he would not eat or drink; and when Circe reproached him he replied that no right-minded man would eat or drink until his companions were released.

Circe took her wand and opened the sty and went among her victims anointing them with a different drug; they became men again, indeed much bigger and more beautiful than before. Odysseus returned to his ship to fetch the rest of his companions. Eurylochus was very reluctant to return to Circe's palace, saying that she would turn them all into pigs or wolves or lions. He insulted Odysseus, who had a good mind to cut his head off, even though he was a kinsman by marriage; but his companions restrained him with soothing words, and they all went back to Circe, now the kindest and most helpful of hostesses.

Such is the narrative in outline. The reader may have noticed one or two faults in the structure and obscurities in the detail; and we should all learn a little more about the art of story-telling in the *Odyssey* if there were time to stop and ask for explanations.

Let us go back to the beginning. Smoke is seen rising from a dwelling in the distance. Somebody must go and see who lives there; and there is much ado about the choice of explorers. Odysseus divides his crew into two companies, one to be led by Eurylochus; lots are drawn, and Eurylochus must go. The motive for this elaborate transaction is quite obvious. We know what is going to happen: men are going to be transformed into pigs; we shall not be satisfied with anything less. But Odysseus himself must be immune: porcine our hero absolutely must not be. 'Pour les yeux modernes', says Gabriel Germain, 'la silhouette du porc évoque des idées comiques et culinaires';[1] and ancient eyes had no very different vision. Moreover, Odysseus is destined to meet Hermes, who will provide him with an antidote to Circe's drugs. If he goes first alone, there will be no transformation at all; if he goes with company, he will know the danger and surely will not imperil his companions. Somebody else must go first, if there is to be any changing into pigs; so there is to be dividing of companions and drawing of lots and the mission of Eurylochus and his half-company.

The details of this episode are unnecessarily lengthy and elaborate; nothing like it occurs in other versions of the story. It would have been enough simply to order some companions to go and explore; three lines sufficed for this whole purpose a few minutes ago, in the story of the Laestrygonians. It seems a pity that the poet should devote so much time to these preliminaries and then greatly abbreviate or even omit certain important parts of the tale which is to follow, as we shall see.

The preliminaries are not even yet complete. Our

story-teller decides that there shall be a survivor who shall report to Odysseus. There is no need of any survivor; in other versions the hero simply wonders why his companions have not returned and goes to look for them. And indeed the survivor is more trouble than he is worth. For he must not be allowed to tell Odysseus the one thing that matters—that his companions have been transformed into pigs. That information is to be given, in the *Odyssey* as in other versions, by the friendly spirit whom the hero will meet on the way. In fact Eurylochus knew nothing about any transformation; he only knew that his companions went indoors and did not come out again. Nevertheless, at the end of the story he speaks as if he had known about the transformation from the beginning: 'She will make them pigs or wolves or lions',[2] he says; in truth he had not known anything about Circe or her powers, and nobody had told him since. But the listener is not, at this late moment, troubled by so small an inconsistency.

It is not immediately apparent why the survivor should be the leader of the company, Eurylochus—'a moonstruck fremescent individual', of bad temper and bad counsel, fitter than most for the sty; and we had rather hoped to see him there. Perhaps he was saved by his standing in society: it may have seemed improper that a kinsman of Odysseus, his second-in-command, should suffer such indignity. Whatever the motive may have been (and I cannot imagine one that satisfies me) a spokesman is promoted from the ranks. Polites, unheard of before or later, earns himself the shadow of a name; he leads the victims to their ludicrous doom, while Eurylochus stays out-of-doors.

Consider now the meeting of Odysseus with Hermes. It is plain that this episode had been fixed in the story long enough for the poet to be able to take certain things for granted. Hermes really meant to inform Odysseus that his companions had been transformed into pigs; what he actually says is quite different: ἔρχαται ὥστε σύες,[3] 'They have been penned in sties *like* pigs', '*as if they were* pigs'. The words implicitly deny that they have been transformed into pigs; only the man who is not a pig can be shut up 'as if he were a pig'. This is simply a fault in the phrasing, and Odysseus assumes that Hermes has asserted what in fact he has implicitly denied, the transformation into pigs. The audience know the story, and know it in this form; nobody will be misled by a careless turn of phrase. The audience is likelier to notice, and to regret, that Hermes does not tell them what Odysseus is to do with the magical plant, the *moly*: 'Take this kindly drug', said Hermes, 'it will avert evil from you; when Circe mixes you her doctored potion, this good drug will save you'.[4] This is very well; but how will it save him? Is he to use the flower or the root or both? How, if at all, should he prepare it? Is it a prophylactic, to be eaten first; or is it an antidote, to be mixed with Circe's brew? Or is he perhaps to make her eat it? 'I will tell you every detail',[5] promised Hermes; and he showed Odysseus the nature of the plant.[6] To us, his audience, he neither shows nor tells anything. We notice and regret this. We notice and regret also that the *moly* is never mentioned again, not even at the time when its powers are needed and presumably employed.

Observe now another curious feature of this scene. Odysseus says that Hermes appeared to him 'in the guise of a young man';[7] and when Hermes has finished speaking, his departure is described as follows: 'Then Hermes went away to great Olympus through the wooded island'.[8] Hermes does not reveal his identity; he was disguised as a young man, and it is a fair question to ask how Odysseus, who is telling the story, knew that he was Hermes, and that when he went away through the wooded island he was in fact on his way to great Olympus. The truth plainly is that this episode has been carelessly transferred from a third-person narrative to a first-person narrative. The poet himself or any of his other characters might describe the departure of Hermes in these terms; make Odysseus the speaker, as here, and the awkwardness is manifest.

In the transactions between Odysseus and Circe there are one or two curious points to be noticed. Odysseus threatens Circe with his sword; she invites him to her bed; he asks, 'How can you ask me to love you when you have changed my friends into pigs?[9] If I am to do as you say, you must first promise that you will not turn me into something degraded and nonhuman when I am undressed'. Next morning he will not eat his breakfast. Circe reproaches him; she has promised not to harm him, and there he sits sulking over untouched porridge. His answer is, in the circumstances, an odd one: how could any right-minded man eat or drink while his friends are still grunting in the sty? It is fair comment to retort, 'Were they not grunting in the sty when you went to bed with Circe last night? Is this the moral code of your right-minded man, that while his friends are in the sty he may share the witch's bed but not her break-fast?' We suspect that the Homeric version here has deviated from a stricter model, in which the release of the companions preceded the hero's amour with the sorceress; and so indeed it did, in the oldest other version known to us.

It is a fair question also to ask what Odysseus means when he says that he is afraid that Circe may make him κακὸν καὶ ἀνήνορα,[10] debased and unmanned, when he is undressed. How can she? Has he not made use of his *moly*? What good are her wand and drugged soup now, even if she takes them to bed with her? What exactly does he fear?

The *Odyssey* takes it for granted that you know a fuller story of which this is an abbreviated version. The tale of the witch in the woods, transformer of humans into birds or beasts or stones or other things, is not uncommon in universal folklore. The Greek epic has adapted it to the adventures of Odysseus, and our poet tells it with as much realism as its nature admits. Given the conventions of the epic, there is not much that might not happen except the turning of men into pigs. This is the heart of the story; it is what we are waiting for. But the poet, unfortunately for us, here as elsewhere in the *Odyssey*, is at pains to minimize the fairytale elements in his story. The transformation into pigs is the one unrealistic element in the tale of Odysseus and Circe; it is therefore reduced to the smallest possible measure. Three times as many lines are given to the killing of a stag for dinner as to the transformation into pigs; and the change back from pigs to men is much too short for our liking. Circe took her wand, but we do not know whether she used it; all we are told is that she 'rubbed another drug on to each one' and that this caused the bristles to drop off their limbs.[11]

Consider now certain other versions of the story, in the hope that they may supply some of the missing links. The following may serve as simple specimens of the folktale which underlies the sophisticated narrative of the *Odyssey*:

(1) One of six brothers met a sorceress in a forest. She dropped a ring. He picked it up and put it on; and 'aussitôt son corps se couvert de poils, deux cornes lui poussèrent, ses oreilles s'allongèrent, et ses deux mains se changèrent en pieds de bouc'. His five brothers came each in turn and suffered the same transformation. They were shut up in a stall. Their sister came to look for them, and with the help of a good fairy outwitted the sorceress. She refused the ring, and killed the sorceress. Her brothers and many other persons recovered their human shape.[12]

(2) One of two brothers met a sorceress in a wood and was turned into stone. The other came to look for him, and being forewarned about the sorceress resisted her enchantments and compelled her to restore his brother and many other persons to human shape.[13]

(3) Nischayadatta, on his way to visit his betrothed, entered a forest accompanied by four men, despite a warning that 'whoever remains there during the night . . . falls a prey to a sorceress who bewilders him, making horns grow on his forehead, and then treats him as a victim and devours him'. Nischayadatta and his companions built a fire in a temple courtyard and prepared to spend the night there. The sorceress 'came there dancing, playing from afar on her lute of bones'; and when she drew near she fixed her eyes on one of the companions and recited a spell. Horns grew on his head, and he 'rose up and danced till he fell in the fire'. The sorceress 'dragged him half-burnt out of the fire and devoured him with delight'. She repeated this performance until all four companions were devoured; then 'being intoxicated with flesh and blood, she laid her lute down on the ground. Thereupon the bold Nischayadatta rose up quickly and seized the lute and

began to play on it, and dancing round with a laugh, to recite that horn-producing charm which he had learnt from hearing it often, fixing his eye at the same time on the face of the sorceress . . . She flung herself prostrate and thus entreated him: Valiant man, do not slay me, a helpless woman . . . Spare me. I know all your story, and will bring about your wish'.[14]

If you look closely you will see that, despite the great and obvious differences of detail, the skeleton of this story is very like the Homeric; and it is now to be observed that in folktales of this type, generally speaking, there are two different types of sorceress: there is the witch who immediately kills (and sometimes eats) any man who comes her way; and there is the beautiful enchantress who is on the look-out for a lover, whom she will turn into an animal, or perhaps kill, after a period of time, when she is tired of him.

The latter type, the sorceress on the look-out for a lover, has a very long pedigree. She appears in one of the oldest works of literature extant today, the *Epic of Gilgamesh*. In that epic the Akkadian goddess Ishtar tries to add Gilgamesh to the list of her lovers:

> Come, Gilgamesh, be thou my lover.
> Do but grant me of thy fruit.
> Thou shalt be my husband and I will be thy wife.
>
> (7)

Gilgamesh replies:

> Which lover didst thou love for ever?
> Which of thy shepherds pleased thee (for all time)?
> Come, and I will name for thee thy lovers . . .
> For Tammuz, the lover of thy youth,

Thou hast ordained wailing year after year.
Having loved the dappled shepherd-bird,
Thou smotest him, breaking his wing . . .
Then thou lovedst a lion, perfect in strength;
Seven pits and seven didst thou dig for him.
Then a stallion thou lovedst, famed in battle;
The whip, the spur, the lash thou ordainedst for him . . .
Then thou lovedst the keeper of the herd . . .
Yet thou smotest him, turning him into a wolf . . .
Then thou lovedst Inshullanu, thy father's gardener . . .
Thou smotest him, turning him into a mole . . .
If thou shouldst love me, thou wouldst (treat me)
    like them.[15]

(42)

So ancient is the pedigree of the supernatural beauty who turns her lovers into animals; and this point of resemblance between the *Odyssey* and the *Epic of Gilgamesh* is perhaps not fortuitous. Babylonian Ishtar may well be the prototype of Homeric Circe. The magician, male or female, is a stranger to Greek legend; and it is presumably significant that the two exceptions who come most readily to mind, Circe and Medea, are at home in the remote Orient, closest to the centers of Akkadian culture. Circe is daughter of the Sun; her island, Aia, is where the Sun rises and Dawn has her palace and dancing-floor.[16] Like the goddesses of the Orient, but not of Greece, she has a sanctuary surrounded by parkland infested by wild animals.

The Ishtar legend is plainly visible again, despite many accretions and complications, in the story of Queen Lab and Bedr Basim as told in the *Arabian Nights*. 'Lab' means 'Sun'; the Arabian sorceress so called has much in common with the Homeric daughter of the Sun,

Circe; and the tale[17] is in general and in several particulars very like that of the *Odyssey*:

Bedr Basim was shipwrecked and carried by a plank[18] to an island with a city near the beach. 'He desired to go up to the city; but there came to him mules and asses and horses, numerous as the grains of sand, and they began to strike him and to prevent his going up from the sea to the city'. In truth they were trying to do him a kindness. They were transf
beautiful sorceress who ruled
for thee lest she should enchar
said to thee by signs, Land nc
thee'.

As Bedr Basim went up to the city he met a friendly sheikh who warned him[20] against the sorceress, Queen Lab: 'Whoever entereth this city, and is a young man like thyself, this infidel enchantress taketh him, and she remaineth with him forty days, and after the forty days she enchanteth him, and he becometh a mule or a horse or an ass'. Bedr Basim passed forty days and nights with Queen Lab. She, like Circe,[21] had female servants who brought fruits and flowers and tables of food and cups of wine. And Bedr Basim, like Odysseus, bathed in the palace, and the queen 'caused him to be clad in the most beautiful apparel'.[22]

On the forty-first night, while Bedr Basim pretended to sleep, the sorceress prepared a magical brew. She gave it to him, and he pretended to eat. Thereupon she splashed water in his face and said, 'Quit this form, O young wretch, O villain, and assume the form of a one-eyed mule of hideous appearance'.[23] But Bedr Basim had got from the friendly sheikh a magical porridge of his own. Unharmed by hers, he induced her to eat his, then splashed water on her face and said, 'Quit this human form, and assume the form of a dappled mule'. And so she did.

The resemblance is close, but there is one big difference: Bedr Basim has no companions. This is a fact which quite alters the character of the story. The Homeric sorceress is one who will transform any man, even the handsomest, at the first encounter; the sorceress of *The Arabian Nights*, like Ishtar in the *Epic of Gilgamesh*, is one who is on the look-out for a lover; she needs only one at a time, and she will not transform him until she is tired of him.

The version of the story most like the *Odyssey* comes from Ceylon. It is told in the seventh chapter of the *Mahāvamsa* (Great History). This is a verse-chronicle in Pāli, based on earlier chronicles and composed early in the sixth century A.D. The composer, Mahānāma, recounts the history of Buddhist Ceylon from the Enlightenment down to the fourth century A.D. The hero of the following story,[24] Vijaya, was the first Buddhist king of Ceylon, where he landed in April 543 B.C., on the day of the Buddha's death:

Prince Vijaya, exiled by his father, arrived in Ceylon accompanied by seven hundred followers. The god Uppalavanna, disguised as a mortal, intercepted him; told him the name of the island; sprinkled magic water on the prince and his companions, and tied prophylactic threads round their arms. He then departed through the air.[25] A servant of the island's enchantress turned himself into a dog and came to meet them. One of the companions, though forbidden by the prince, followed the dog, saying that if there is a dog, there must be a village hereabout. He found the sorceress sitting under a tree beside a pond, spinning thread.[26] He bathed in the pond and drank water from it. 'And while he was taking roots and water from that tank, she started up and thus addressed him: "Stop, thou art my prey". The man, as if he was spell-bound, stood without the power of moving. By the virtue of the charmed thread, she was not able to devour him'. So she 'cast him bellowing into a subterraneous abode'.[27] The rest of the seven hundred companions came each in turn and suffered the same fate. Vijaya set out in search of them. He saw the enchantress and guessed what she had done. 'Pray, why dost thou not produce my ministers?' said he. 'Prince', she replied, 'from ministers what pleasure canst thou derive? Do drink and bathe ere thou departest'. The prince rushed at her; seized her throat with one hand and her hair with the other; then 'raising his sword with his right hand he exclaimed, Slave, restore me my followers, or I will put thee to death'.[28] She begged for mercy: 'Lord, spare my life; on thee will I confer this sovereignty; unto thee will I render the favours of my sex; and every other service according to thy desire'.[29] The resemblance to the *Odyssey* is very close at this point; closer still in what follows, for Prince Vijaya, 'in order that he might not be involved in a similar difficulty again', made the sorceress 'take an oath'.[30]

The sorceress immediately released the companions: 'These men must be famished', she said; and she 'distributed rice and a vast variety of other articles procured from the wrecked ships of mariners who had fallen a prey to her'. Then she 'transformed herself into a girl of sixteen years of age, and decorating her person with innumerable ornaments . . . and approaching him, quickly inflamed the passion of the chief . . . Foreseeing all the future advantages that were to result to him, he passed the night with her'.

Vijaya became king; the sorceress came to a bad end.

The chapter ends with the customary subscription, 'The seventh chapter in the Mahawamso, . . . composed equally to delight and to afflict righteous men'.

The resemblance to the Homeric story is close not only in outline but also in a few of the smaller details; and some are quite sure that Homer was the source, or one of the sources, for the *Mahāvamsa*. To me, the notion of Homeric influence on such a history of Buddhist Ceylon in the early centuries of the Christian era, or earlier, appears in the highest degree improbable; and I would point to the differences, in particular one of the differences, between the two versions. First, the Homeric motif of the magical plant, *moly*, is very unlike that of the prophylactic water-sprinkling and arm-threads in the *Mahāvamsa*. Secondly, in the *Mahāvamsa* the release of the companions precedes (as it ought to) the amour of the hero and the sorceress; this is surely an older version than Homer's. Thirdly, and most significant, the *Mahāvamsa* has no transformation into pigs or any other animals. The companions of Vijaya are simply shut up in a cave; they are not transformed at all. It is very unlikely that this motif, the turning of men into pigs, which has made the Homeric story memorable for all time, would have been omitted by any later version composed under the influence of the *Odyssey*. It is much likelier that the *Odyssey* and the *Mahāvamsa* have the same ultimate source; if so, that source may be a story told in the remotest past, before the separation of the Indo-European peoples into their Indian and their European branches; the story of the Arrow and the Axes, common to the *Odyssey* and the old Indian epics, will keep it company.

This explanation may be confirmed by the survival of the word μῶλυ in this context. The word was not preserved elsewhere in Greek (later writers have it from Homer); but some believe that it did survive in the Sanskrit of the old Indian epics, *mulam*,[31] 'root'. Homer has it here simply because it had always been fixed in this part of this story. It was never forgotten that the antidotal herb in the Indo-European tale had always been called by this and no other name. The Indians preserved the word, the Greeks did not—except in the tale of Odysseus and Circe.

The final episode in the *Odyssey*, the hero's sudden attack, the sorceress' plea for mercy and promise of her favors, is a motif as old as anything in folklore. There is not much difference, except of detail, between *Odyssey* 10.321–335 and the Akkadian tale of Nergal and Ereshkigal,[32] which goes back to the second millenium B.C. if not to the third:

Nergal alone of the gods failed to respect the queen of the underworld, Ereshkigal. He was sent down to make his peace with her. She intended to kill him, but just when she thought he was at her mercy

> he took hold of Ereshkigal,
> By her hair he brought her down from the throne
> To the ground, to cut off her head.
> 'Kill me not, brother, let me speak a word to thee'.
> When Nergal heard her, his hands relaxed.
> She weeps, humbled:
> 'Be thou my husband, and I will be thy wife'.
>
> (76)

The oddest matter in the Homeric version was that of the *moly*, the herbal charm against the spells of Circe. Magically medicinal herbs have always been familiar enough. Who is unaware (for example) that poachers in Bohemia render themselves invulnerable by swallowing the seed from a fir-cone found growing upwards before sunrise on St. John's day; or that the root of the yellow mullein, dug up in silence with a ducat on midsummer eve and worn in linen next to the skin, preserves the wearer from epilepsy?[33] The audience would guess at once what sort of plant the *moly* is; nor would they be surprised to hear that it was 'hard for men to dig up'. It was common knowledge that nobody who valued his life would attempt to dig up the 'baaras' in Palestine, bryony in Armenia, or the mandrake anywhere.[34] For the uprooting of these, and of the *aglaophotis*, or peony, you needed an expendable dog. Thus Aelian on the peony: 'No one digs round it or uproots it. The first man to lay hands on it in ignorance of its nature died almost immediately. What you need is a strong dog, starved for several days. Tie a noose round the foot of the peony, and attach the other end to the dog. Set a plate of meat, cooked and strong-smelling, in front of the dog. The dog will rush at the meat, and its movement will uproot the peony. The moment the roots are out of the ground, the dog will expire'.[35]

So much might be taken for granted; and it is obvious that our poet is recounting a long familiar tale. It is nevertheless surprising, and much to be regretted, that he refrains from telling us (however briefly) what Odysseus is to do with the *moly*; and still more surprising that Odysseus should in fact do nothing with it. Only a dozen lines come between the description of the *moly* and the occasion for its use by Odysseus; yet it is already wholly forgotten. This matter of the hero's antidote is so variously treated in other versions of the story that we get no help from them.

Consider, for example, the account given in the Sanskrit story of Bhímaparákrama.[36] Bhímaparákrama took
lodgings with a sorceress. 'Being tired, I slept for some
time, but then I woke up, and out of curiosity I remained
quiet, and watched her, and while I was watching the
woman took a handful of barley, and sowed it all about
inside the house, her lips trembling all the time with
muttering spells. Those grains of barley immediately
sprang up, and produced ears, and ripened, and she cut
them down and parched them and ground them and
made them into a barley-meal. And she sprinkled the
barley-meal with water and put it into a brass pot, and,
after arranging the house as it was before, she went out'.

So far the parallel to the *Arabian Nights* is close; but
this hero, unlike Odysseus and Bedr Basim, has no antidote of his own. He can only improvise: 'Taking that
meal out of the brass pot, I transferred it to the meal-
bin, and I took as much barley out of the meal-bin, and
placed it in the brass vessel, taking care not to mix the
two kinds. Then I went back again to bed, and the
woman came in and roused me up, and gave me that
meal from the brass pot to eat, and she ate some herself,
taking what she ate from the meal-bin, and so she ate
the charmed meal, not knowing that I had exchanged
the two kinds. The moment she had eaten that barley-
meal, she became a she-goat'.

The detail of the manner in which the hero neutralizes
the magical arts of the sorceress is, as a rule, treated at
some length in versions other than the *Odyssey*; as
indeed we expect it to be, for the hero's life, at least in
human shape, depends upon it. The matter is wholly
omitted by Homer; yet he will devote two dozen lines
to the purely ornamental description of Circe's hand-
maidens waiting on Odysseus, and the provision of

venison for dinner takes about thirty lines. There must be a reason for this apparent disproportion; the most obvious and likely explanation is to be found in the poet's desire to suppress the purely magical elements in the folktales which have been adopted by the story of Odysseus.

The stories of Bedr Basim and Bhímaparákrama focus our attention again on a point mentioned earlier: the two variations of the basic theme. In one, the hero has companions who are transformed or devoured or otherwise maltreated by the sorceress; he alone survives, and either kills the sorceress or (more or less) marries her. In the other the sorceress is a beautiful demon on the look-out for a lover; the hero spends a certain time with her, and when she is tired of him she transforms him. There is no reason why these two different types of demon should not be combined in one person; and so indeed they are in both *Odyssey* and *Mahāvamsa*. If they are combined, it is better that the release of the companions should precede the beginning of the amour, as in the *Mahāvamsa* but not in the *Odyssey*; and it is most natural that the hero's successful resistance to his own transformation should precede the beginning of the amour, as in both the Indian and the Greek epics. But it looks as though both the *Odyssey* and the *Mahāvamsa* show awareness of the variation of the story exemplified in the *Epic of Gilgamesh* and the *Arabian Nights*. The hero who beds with the enchantress must expect that one night when she is tired of him she will concoct a potion or devise some other mischief while he sleeps; and both Odysseus and Prince Vijaya make the sorceress swear a great and—in their circumstances—unnecessary oath that she will do nothing of the kind. It was, I suppose, common knowledge that the hero who sleeps with the sorceress is at great risk. There was in fact no apparent reason for fear in either the Greek or the Indian epic, because the magical arts of the sorceress have already been neutralized before the love-affair begins; but the poet and his audience know other stories where this was not so—where the danger comes at the end of the love-affair. The strong oath demanded by Odysseus is a reminder of what might have been.

I have already said that one of the most remarkable features of the Homeric tale of Circe is the contrast between the length and detail of unimportant passages and the rapid and superficial treatment of such interesting matters as the use of the *moly* and the transformation into and out of pigs. The poet has done his best to reduce the magical to a minimum; but his best was not good enough for the delicate nerves of posterity. The author of the treatise *On the Sublime* is admired by some as an acute and sensitive critic. He reveres Homer above all men; but when he reads about Aeolus with his bag of winds or Circe turning men into pigs, he cannot conceal his sorrow and disapproval. These things, he says, are flotsam found only on the ebbtide of greatness; they are the work of an elderly man astray in the realm of the fabulous and the incredible. He mentions them only to show 'how easily great natures in their decline are sometimes diverted into absurdity'.[37] The spikiest of his predecessors, most atrabiliar of croaking men, one Zoilus, had made fun of the victims of Circe, calling them 'whimpering piglets';[38] and our sublime friend with the delicate nerves finds this fair comment.

IV

Aeolus; the Cattle of the Sun;
and the Sirens

IV Circe and the Laestrygonians are creatures of folktale; the tales of Aeolus and of the Cattle of the Sun are different in this respect. The heart and soul of these two stories, the motifs which are the mainsprings of their action, come from life, not folklore. The bag of winds and the holy cattle are familiar to the audience from contemporary experience. Both stories are realistic and credible from start to finish. Take, first, the story of Aeolus and his bag of winds:

Odyssey 10.1–76: Odysseus escaped from the Cyclops and sailed to the island of Aeolus, an island not fixed but floating on the sea. There lived Aeolus in a strongly fortified and comfortable palace, with his nameless wife and six sons married to six daughters. He entertained Odysseus hospitably, and was obliging when, at the end of a month, Odysseus asked for help homewards.

Aeolus had made a bag out of an oxhide: 'and in it he tied up the tracks of the storm-winds, because Zeus had made him steward of the winds, to start or stop any one of them he wished. He tied up the bag with a silver cord in the hollow ship, so that there should not be the least breath of contrary wind; and for me he set the west wind to blow, to drive the ship and ourselves. But he was not destined to fulfill this; we were ruined by our own folly'.

They sailed for nine days, and came in sight of Ithaca: 'And then sweet slumber overcame me, for I was tired out. I had been handling the sheet of the ship all the time, not giving it to any other companion, so that we might come home the quicker'. While Odysseus slept, his companions took the opportunity to tell each other of their suspicions. They had their eyes on that silver-corded sack. They were nearly home after years of dangerous travel, but empty-handed; and here surely was a bag of gold and silver, and no word of a share for them. 'So they undid the sack, and out jumped all the winds, and at once a tempest caught them and carried them out to sea, loud-lamenting, away from their native land. And I woke up, and pondered in my blameless heart, whether to throw myself overboard and perish in the sea, or to endure in silence and remain among the living'.

They were driven all the way back to the island of Aeolus. Odysseus felt humiliated. Aeolus was at dinner with his wife and twelve children; they were astonished to see Odysseus and his companions arrive and sit down by the door-post. They asked why he had returned; had they not given him a friendly send-off to his homeland or wherever else he liked? 'So they spoke; and I, heart-broken, cried out among them, "They have ruined me, my accursed companions, and, besides, my wretched sleepiness."' There was silence at the dinner-table; then Aeolus spoke: '"Begone from the island with all speed, most criminal of creatures; it would be a wrong deed for me to give conveyance or send-off to the man who is hated by the blessed gods . . ." That is what he said as he dismissed me from his house; and I groaned heavily, and we were all heart-broken, and sailed away from the place'.

I have called this story realistic and credible from start to finish. All over the world, in all ages of history, men have tried to find means of controlling the weather, especially rain and wind. More than fifty examples of methods employed to control the wind may be read in *The Golden Bough*,[1] most of them magical and some of them very elaborate: 'When a Haida Indian wishes to obtain a fair wind, he fasts, shoots a raven, singes it in the fire, and then going to the edge of the sea sweeps it over the surface four times in the direction in which he wishes the wind to blow. He then throws the raven behind him, but afterwards picks it up and sets it in a sitting posture at the foot of a spruce-tree, facing towards the required wind. Propping its beak open with a stick, he requests a fair wind for a certain number of days; then going away he lies covered up in a mantle till another Indian asks him for how many days he has desired the wind, which question he answers'.[2] It is then safe for him to sail. Procedures of this kind, more or less elaborate, are the norm for rain-makers and wind-controllers in primitive societies. Some of them suppose the wind to be, or to be the work of, a supernatural being, commonly a demon who must be frustrated by the arts of the magician. It is, as a rule, the more civilized society which ascribes the origin and control of natural phenomena to intelligent divinities; believes that the gods may be influenced by human action and behavior; constructs a religious system; and creates a priesthood with ritual procedures for direct intercession with the gods.

The story of Aeolus combines the religious with the magical approach to nature. Ritual worship of the winds was practiced in Mycenaean Greece; the Linear B tablets[3] tell us of the Mycenaeans' priestess, *anemon ijereia*, who will pray to the winds and appease them with worship and sacrifice. It would be impious to suppose that the wind-gods cannot send a favorable wind or recall a storm if they think fit, or that they will not listen to prayer, though they may have reason not to accede to it. So ancient is the worship of the winds in Greece.

Now Homer knows nothing of Mycenaean wind-gods; Aeolus is not of their family. He is indeed not divine. He has a human father, Hippotes; but he happens to be a friend of the gods, φίλος ἀθανάτοισι θεοῖσι, and Zeus has appointed him steward of the winds, with power to start or stop any one of them he wishes. Thus the function of Aeolus in the *Odyssey* is essentially Olympian-religious; he has an office within the government of Zeus. His method, on the other hand, is purely magical, of a type common in primitive societies, a variation on the theme of singed ravens propped up under spruce-trees, though much simpler and more convincing. It is indeed a wholly credible method. The bag of winds belongs not to folklore but to life, a particular sphere of life in which magical arts are commonly employed. It may be used as a motif in folktale or adventure story, but its proper place is in the home of a familiar citizen, the magician at the dockside, whose customers are the sailor and the fisherman.

The sale of devices to control the winds has been common for ages throughout the world. The one most like the bag of Aeolus is the knotted cord or cloth which contains the winds in its knots. Each knot may contain a different wind; or the force of the same wind may depend on the number of knots untied. 'Shetland seamen', says Frazer, 'still buy winds in the shape of knotted handkerchieves';[4] and they and their neighbors have been practicing this method for a very long time. Jacob Grimm quotes a story of the wind-selling inhabitants of Vinlandia, taken from a work composed about the year 1360:[5]

'It is a barbarian people, savage and wild, devoted to magical arts. They offer and sell "winds at a price" to men who sail to their coasts or to those who are long delayed among them through failure of the wind. They make a ball of thread and tie various knots in it, and tell the sailors to extract from the ball up to three knots or more, according to the extent to which they wish to have the wind stronger'. The more knots they extract from the ball, the greater the wind. The gods amuse themselves from time to time by making the wind strong enough to sink the ship.

The following story,[6] which has much in common with Homer's, looks more like folktale. It is not in fact a folktale. Its substance is based on common experience, and is represented as true; no doubt its form owes something to art:

'In Siseby on the Schlei dwelt a woman skilled in sorcery, who could turn the wind round. The herring-fishermen of Schleswig often used to land there. On one occasion they wanted to return to Schleswig, but the wind was in the west. So they asked the woman to turn the wind round. She said she would, in return for a plate of fish; so the fishermen offered her herrings, perch, bream, and pike, these being all the fish they had. Thereupon she gave them a cloth with three knots, and said that they could open the first and second knots, but must not open the third till they reached land. The fishermen spread their sails, although the wind was still in the west; but the moment the oldest member of the company opened the first knot, a fair wind came from the east. He opened the second knot, and a strong wind came upon them, and they reached their town at high speed. And now they were curious to know what would happen if they opened the third knot too: they had hardly done so, when a terrible hurricane fell upon them from the west; they had to jump into the water in a hurry, to drag their ship to the beach'.

Whether you tie up all the winds together in a bag or each wind separately in a knot along a cord or cloth, the principle is much the same. There are many regions of the seafaring world in which such practices have been recorded; the story of Aeolus suggests that they were familiar to Greeks in the time of Homer.

As a rule, the professional wind-seller behaves as sole proprietor of his business, not as agent for divine powers instructing him. The Norwegian lady[7] who could (so she said) sink a ship by opening a sack containing a storm-wind, was in absolute control of her business, which she conducted at home among her neighbours. Whencesoever the magician acquires his powers, once acquired they are his own. The setting is purely magical, not (as a rule) religious. Procedures are more complicated, and of a different kind, if the powers rest not with a local magician who can sell you a knotted cloth of his own making across the counter, but with a god or demon who may need a home on earth, as well as in Heaven, and a priesthood and a cult. Such was the gloomy fetish Bagba, who lived on the top of Mount Agu in Togoland, attended by a priest who had a stock of winds shut up in large pots.[8]

The Homeric audience would find nothing in the story of Aeolus outside their own experience. Floating islands were common in the Mediterranean. We disapprove of daughters marrying sons; but these had no other choice. Bags of winds or similar equipment could surely be bought in foreign ports, probably in Greek ports too. Did not the great philosopher Empedocles, ablest of men, in a much more sophisticated age, catch winds in bags made of donkey-skin, to protect the harvest from the Etesians?[9]

Nor is there any element of unreality in the story of the sacred Cattle of the Sun:[10]

Odyssey 12.260–425: Odysseus escaped from Scylla and Charybdis, and very soon came to an island called 'Thrinacia', inhabited only by the sacred cattle and sheep of the Sun and their herdswomen, two daughters of the Sun. These cattle were immortal and without progeny. There were seven herds of cattle, seven flocks of sheep, fifty animals in each herd or flock; so seven hundred animals altogether. Circe and Teiresias had warned Odysseus not to harm them, on pain of death; so he told his companions to drive on past the island. But the chief of them, Eurylochus, persuaded them to pass the night ashore. Very well, said Odysseus; only swear me a strong oath, all of you, that you will not kill cattle or sheep on the island, but be satisfied with the food which Circe gave us. They swore the strong oath and landed and ate their dinner. But next day came a wind against them out of the south and east. For a whole month it blew. Their provisions ran out; they ate what fish and birds they could, but they began to starve.

One day Odysseus went inland to pray; and there he fell asleep. Eurylochus took his chance to do mischief. His behavior in the story of Circe was foolish; it was fatal here. 'Let us go', he said, 'and chase the best of the Sun's cows, and sacrifice them to the immortals who dwell in the wide sky. If we get back to our native land of Ithaca, the first thing we will do is to build a rich temple to the Sun and put many fine ornaments in it. If the Sun is so angry about his cattle, and intends to destroy our ship, and the other gods follow him, I would rather gulp at the sea-water and lose my life once for all than suffer slow torture on a desert island'.

They killed some cattle and cooked them and made

all ready for dinner; Odysseus could smell the cooking as he returned to the camp. The daughters of the Sun told their father, who complained to Zeus, refusing to shine on earth ever again unless avenged. Zeus promised to destroy the ship as soon as it put to sea again.[11]

The fatal dinner was eaten, not without omens of most black and odious import: the cow-skins got up and walked about; flesh mooed on the spits both before and after cooking. For six days the men ate the mooing meat, choosing the best cattle. On the seventh day the storm-wind fell, and they put to sea. As soon as they were out of sight of land, Zeus fulfilled his promise to the Sun. The ship was smashed; the steersman's head was broken by the falling mast; the rest were drowned. Odysseus alone escaped, riding the sea on the ship's keel.

This is a simple tale; no part of it would strain the credulity of the Homeric audience. It was nothing new to them that animals should be under divine protection. It was common knowledge that the Sun had flocks of holy sheep at Cape Tainaron in South Laconia[12] and at Apollonia in northwestern Greece,[13] and a herd of holy cows at Gortyn in Crete.[14] Nor were those dismal omens beyond belief. Cow-skins walking and flesh mooing on spits are not normal; but three hundred years later the more sophisticated audience of Herodotus[15] will accept a similar miracle recorded almost, if not quite, within their own lifetime: Artaÿctes, a Persian governor, had committed sacrilege by rifling the tomb of the Mycenaean hero Protesilaos. One day, when he was a prisoner of the Greeks, a miracle occurred: one of his warders was frying dried fish; and the dried fish suddenly began to leap and wriggle in the pan like fish newly caught. The warders were astonished; Artaÿctes was not. 'This portent', he said, 'is not for you but for me. It means that Protesilaos, though dead and dry, has power from Heaven to take vengeance on the man who wronged him'. And so he had; the barbarous killing of Artaÿctes followed very soon. Another example, very like the Homeric, from the third century B.C.:[16] 'certain oxen were sacrificed; and their heads, while lying at a distance from their bodies, were seen to put out their tongues and lick round their own blood'. That was an evil omen for King Pyrrhus; and his death followed quickly.

The sacred cow is a very ancient animal, to be found in the most diverse regions of the earth. In Egypt,[17] for example, the cow was sacred to Isis; on no account might one be killed or even maltreated, let alone eaten. No Egyptian (says Herodotus, 2.41) would kiss a Greek, dreading the pollution of beef-stained lips. There is an obvious reason for this rule. In India, the Hindu law-givers at a very early date recognized 'that these animals were particularly valuable in a country where there is no other beast available for tilling or for transporting...' Moreover, 'the milk was an indispensable addition to the food of the multitude of poor natives'. Hindu law therefore gave divine protection to the cow, so that 'to eat the flesh of the cow is an ineffaceable defilement', and 'to kill a cow...is not only a crime but an awful sacrilege, a deicide, which can only be expiated by the death of the offender'.[18]

It is thus plain that the Cattle of the Sun in the *Odyssey* are not, for Homer's audience, creatures of folktale, like Circe and the Cyclops and the Laestrygonians. The story has nothing magical in it; nothing unreal; nothing for the poet to suppress or hurry over. It is a realistic adventure story, built round a motif which has its origin not in any kind of fiction but in a fact of contemporary life. Though the idea of the sacred cow, in the Egyptian or Indian sense, is not Greek, the idea that the sun-god possessed herds of cattle and flocks of sheep, whose killing would surely be avenged, was familiar throughout Greek lands. It was then easy for the poet to transfer such a herd to a remote island and to make its inviolability the mainspring of his realistic narrative.

It remains nevertheless possible that the use of this motif in folktale or adventure story was older than the *Odyssey*, and that Homer, here as elsewhere, has adopted a ready-made tale, putting Odysseus in the place of the nameless or named hero of a popular story. I know of only one really close parallel to Homer's account of the Cattle of the Sun: it comes from the *Danish History* of Saxo Grammaticus,[19] who wrote in the reign of Waldemar II, 1202–1241. The first nine books of the *Danish History* cover the early period up to the year 936; their contents are mainly legendary. The last seven books cover the years 936 to 1202, and are intended to be historical. The following story is told in the legendary part:

Gormo, son of King Harold, led an expedition of three hundred men in three ships, with Thorkill as guide, in search of the land of Geruth, in the perpetual darkness which prevails beyond the limits of the ocean, a land said to be full of treasure. They met adverse weather, and their provisions ran out. They were not far from starvation when they sighted an island, where they disembarked.

'Now Thorkill forbade them to kill more of the cattle, of which great numbers were running about on the shore, than would suffice to appease their hunger just once; otherwise the gods who protected the place would prevent them from leaving. But the sailors were more inclined to consider the continued satisfying of their hunger than to listen to this prohibition; they paid less attention to their safety than to the temptation of their bellies, and they filled the empty spaces of their ships with slaughtered cattle.' During the night they were attacked by giants, who surrounded their ships. 'One of them, bigger than the others and armed with a mighty cudgel, actually walked across the sea; and when he got closer, he began to shout that they would not escape until they had atoned for the wrong they had done by slaughtering the cattle; they must make good the damage they had done to the sacred animals, by giving up a man from each of the three ships. Thorkill yielded to these threats and gave up three men chosen by lot'.

Here we find the Homeric story in its folktale dress. These Danish adventurers are looking for treasure in a land beyond the known limits of the world; and the guardians of the sacred cattle are dreadful monsters, not comely and credible daughters of the Sun. There is no means of telling whether a popular tale of this kind, with similar appurtenances of folklore, was current in Greece before Homer and known to him.

Consider finally the mysterious episode of the Sirens.[20] Circe described to Odysseus the dangers of the way back from her island to his home in Ithaca:

Odyssey 12.39–54: 'First you will come to the Sirens, who enchant every man who comes to them. If anyone approaches unaware and hears the voice of the Sirens, he never returns home for wife and child to stand beside him and rejoice; the Sirens, sitting in their meadow, enchant him with their melodious song. And around them is a great heap of the bones of men putrefying, their skins shrivelling about them. So drive straight on past, and soften honeysweet wax and rub it into your companions' ears, so that none of the others may listen. For yourself, if you wish to listen, let them bind you, hand and foot, in the swift ship, upright in the mast-step, and let ropes be fastened from the mast, so that you can enjoy listening to the twin Sirens' voice. But if you should implore your companions and command them to release you, then let them bind you with still more fastenings'.

When the ship came near to the Sirens, Odysseus repeated these instructions to his companions. We are told again of the flowery meadow the Sirens live in; and we learn that it is an island.

The companions did as they were told. They allowed Odysseus to stop their ears with wax, and they tied him to the mast. Now when the ship was as close to the island as a voice could carry, the Sirens began their song:

Odyssey 12.184–191: 'Come this way, renowned Odysseus, great glory of the Achaeans. Stop your ship, so that you may listen to our voice. For no man yet has driven past here in his black ship before listening to the sweet sound of music from our lips, but full of pleasure he goes home, knowing more than he ever did. Because we know everything, all that the Argives and Trojans suffered in wide Troy by the will of God; we know everything that happens all over the fruitful earth'.

Odysseus wished to hear more, and signalled to his companions. But they tied him still more tightly, until they were out of reach of the Sirens' voices. Then they unstopped their ears and untied Odysseus.

Who were the Sirens? '"Why, the truth is, my dear," said Mr Pecksniff, smiling upon his assembled kindred, "that I am at a loss for a word. The name of those fabulous animals (pagan, I regret to say) who used to sing in the water, has quite escaped me." Mr George Chuzzlewit suggested "Swans". "No", said Mr Pecksniff. "Not swans. Very like swans, too. Thank you". The nephew with the outline of a countenance, speaking for the first and last time on that occasion, propounded "Oysters". "No", said Mr Pecksniff . . . "nor oysters. But by no means unlike oysters; a very excellent idea; thank you, my dear Sir, very much. Wait! Sirens. Dear me! Sirens, of course"'.[21]

Mr Pecksniff understood a Siren to be a female whose charms lure a man to destruction; and that is what the word means today in many a language. It is a rare word in Greek poetry after Homer; where it occurs, it almost always reflects the Homeric Sirens, meaning either a female of dangerous and deceitful charm,[22] or simply one who sings beautifully, without any notion of danger or deceit.[23] The Greeks knew nothing about the Homeric Sirens except what they found in the *Odyssey*; but they who looked so coldly on the Lotus-Eaters embraced the Sirens warmly, and were quick to supply them with a parentage, with individual names,[24] with a geographical location, and with an end to their story.

Their father was Phorcus;[25] or you may prefer Achelous.[26] Their mother was Earth,[27] if she was not Sterope[28] or one of the Muses.[29] Concerning their home there was general agreement: they inhabited three island-rocks off the west coast of Italy, between Sorrento and Capri.[30] As for the end of their story, it was fated that they must die if their charms ever failed to attract a passing vessel to its destruction;[31] this happened once in the story of Odysseus[32] and once in the story of the Argonauts.[33]

Now there is something mysterious about all this. For everybody knew, from the beginning to the end of Greek history, what a Siren really was; and the Siren they knew seems to bear no resemblance whatsoever to the so-called Sirens of the *Odyssey*. There are many works of art from the eighth century B.C. onwards to tell us the dismal truth about these creatures.[34] We know them well. They are demons of the underworld. The Siren is not a beautiful female, but a bird with a human head. It sings no enchanting melody, though it may croak a dirge for the dead at the bidding of Pluto or Persephone.[35] It lives not in a flowery meadow[36] on a remote island, but in the gloom of Hades.[37] It does not lure men to destruction; it waits (impatiently, perhaps) until you die, then escorts your soul (gently or violently) on its journey to the underworld. Its effigy often crowns the tomb, presumably representing the soul of the departed.[38]

So strong is the contrast between the real Siren, familiar to us all, and the romantic Siren portrayed by Homer. Yet the ancients appear to have found nothing amiss. The name of this dismal and dreadful human-headed fowl is simply transferred in the *Odyssey* to the enchantresses of a well-known folktale; and the artist[39] and the writer are ready to accept that the Sirens in Homer are the same creatures as the familiar demons who are waiting in the underworld for our death. Why did nobody ever say, 'It is nonsense to give this name, which stands for something wholly different, to the enchanting females of the folktale'?

The transfer of the name 'Sirens' might seem even stranger if the episode in Homer is indeed taken from common folklore. If everybody knew what a Siren really was (and there is no doubt about that), and if everybody already knew the story of the females who lure mariners to destruction, then surely the transfer of the name should have been the more noticeable and surprising? It is therefore appropriate now to enquire whether the episode is taken from common folklore; and the answer is quickly given.

The episode of the Sirens in the *Odyssey* is an adaptation of an old and widespread folktale.[40] The bird-woman, whose music enchants the traveller, is to be found in the early Buddhist art of Java,[41] where, late in the nineteenth century, men still dreaded the *pragangan*, 'the beautiful genii in female form, who abide on the banks of rivers ... exercise upon men a bewitching fascination, disturb their mental faculties, and render them mad'.[42] Nearer home, but certainly not of Homeric pedigree, are the Sirens of Mecklenburg: 'About the hour of midnight on nights of the full moon, the *Watermömen* sing in the ponds. Their song is glorious and alluring, but whoever attends to it is drawn by them into the water and must remain with them. Near Rehna there is a pond, the so-called Dead Sea ... which had the reputation of being the abode of the *Watermömen* and often claimed victims'.[43] 'In an Irish tale the Druids advise the travellers to close their ears with wax to avoid the fascinations of the mermaids'.[44] The fishermen of Brittany and Malta have long been familiar with mermaids who entice them to destruction by the sweetness of their voices. The Siren of Brittany 'est belle comme le jour, elle chante comme un ange'; 'if you stop to listen to her, you will forget father, mother, wife, and children'.[45] In the waters about Malta and Gozo the Siren is 'wonderfully beautiful, never grows old, and is full of tricks'. Her 'voice is glorious'. She is 'a good friend to the sharks, and makes them a present of the victims of her enchantment'.[46]

The Homeric Sirens have much in common also with the females in a story from the Pāli *Jātaka* (Birth-Stories of Buddha). A traveller is told of the dangers that await him in a remote region: 'There is peril on the road thither, in journeying through a great forest . . . Ogres have their dwelling therein, and ogresses make villages and houses arise by the wayside . . . Arrayed in celestial splendour the ogresses sit within their abodes, seducing wayfarers with honied words: "Weary you seem", they say, "come hither, and eat and drink before you journey further on your way" . . . And they ensnare men's senses, captivating the sense of beauty with utter loveliness, the ear with sweet minstrelsy . . .' When you have made love to them, they eat you.[47]

It is easy to demonstrate that the story of the beautiful female whose singing lures the traveller, and especially the seafarer, to destruction, is common and widespread. I therefore suppose that the narrative in the *Odyssey* is based on familiar folktale, not free invention.[48] And it is the content of the common folktale which explains why the poet might call his females 'Sirens', and why the ancients found nothing amiss with this transfer of the name.

The truth will be that the *Odyssey*[49] has abbreviated and modified the common folktale, yet not so far as to make it unrecognizable. The audience know the folktale, and recognize it immediately in the Homeric narrative. They know also that the females in the folktale are much more like the underworld demons whom they call 'Sirens' than they appear to be in Homer. They already know, and take for granted, all that Homer omits. In the familiar folktale the enchantresses may have been, as they often are, demons masquerading as maidens;[50] they may very well have been killers and even cannibals, as in some other versions.[51] They may have been, as often in other versions, not wholly of human shape; though they do not belong to the lower world, they are certainly not normal creatures of the upper world. Of all this Homer says nothing, one way or the other; it was not necessary that he should say anything, for his audience knew it all. And they were quite prepared to accept the transference of the name 'Sirens'; for are not the females in the common folktale also, like the real Sirens, supernatural, monstrous, and greatly to be feared?

The allusiveness of Homer's narrative, and the abbreviation, are evident especially in the lines about the victims of the Sirens: 'Around them is a great heap of the bones of men putrefying, their skins shrivelling about them'. What had happened to these men? Just how did the Sirens kill their victims?

Surely not by shipwreck: 'The breeze had dropped', says Odysseus, 'and there was a windless calm; a *daimon* had laid the waves to rest'.[52] We notice that the bones are not (as they would have been in some other versions) the bones of men eaten by the Sirens: they are putrefying, and the skin is still upon them, though shrivelling. In the familiar folktale the victims of the Sirens died somehow: Homer suppresses the mode of their death and excludes the common motifs of shipwreck and cannibalism. We cannot guess, but the audience knows the true answer (whatever it may be) and will remember. These are dangerous creatures, surely akin to Empousa or the Harpies.[53] 'Sirens', the poet calls them; not what is usually understood by the term, but like enough. Have you any reason to doubt that on some remote island real Sirens might be found, on earth instead of under it, singing sweet music instead of dismal dirges, intent on killing you instead of waiting for your death and then carrying your body off?

So much for the Sirens. I suppose I ought to end these chapters with a general summary of findings; but in truth I have not been much concerned to find anything. I have simply indulged a desire to linger in the Odyssean land of ogres and Lotus-Eaters, of Sirens and sorceresses. Living among them and going close to them, I seem to see behind them and beyond them. Backgrounds became visible, in some places less dimly than in others. I have tried to sketch the outlines of what lies beyond. The figures in the foreground look different, and (to me, at least) more interesting when the backgrounds have been painted in.

One thing at least is plain: the Greeks in remotest antiquity, like the Greeks of modern times, revelled in folktales. The Homeric version of these tales is always abbreviated and allusive. It assumes that the full story is known to the audience. Greeks at all times had an insatiable hunger for their traditional myths and legends; it now looks as though the telling of a quite different sort of story, of which there is not much other trace in the early period, was common among the diversions of their domestic and social lives in the long Dark Age—the telling of tales about ogres and witches, the adventures of imaginary heroes and heroines in the world of fancy, stories of

> fairy elves,
> Whose midnight revels by a forest side
> Or fountain some belated peasant sees,
> Or dreams he sees, while overhead the Moon
> Sits arbitress.[54]

There remains, however, the possibility that Homer's source was not contemporary but traditional. It is certain that some of his folktales were already familiar to his audience through an epic poem on the Argonauts' quest for the Golden Fleece; and there is no knowing how far back such blending of saga and folktale may go. For a short time, indeed, I entertained a hope that I might conclude by tracing the Sirens and the dog-headed monster called 'Scylla' a long way back, to an ultimate source in Minoan Crete; that I might show you pictures not only of a sub-Minoan Siren on a sherd from Praisos in eastern Crete but also of a Minoan Scylla on a clay-sealing from Knossos and perhaps another on the silver siege-vase. The truth is less romantic. The sub-Minoan Siren is in fact a Geometric Greek. As for the creature on the clay-sealing which was to be identified with the dog-headed Scylla, Professor Spyridon Marinatos took a closer look, and detected—of all things—a hippopotamus.[55]

Appendix
The Arrow
and
the Axes

At the end of the nineteenth book of the *Odyssey* Penelope tells Odysseus, whom she has not yet recognized, that she can no longer postpone surrender to the Suitors. These are her words, in the plainest English:

I will tell you another thing, and do you take it to heart: it is already on the way, that hateful morning which shall divorce me from Odysseus' house. For I shall now set up a competition—those axes, which Odysseus used to stand in a line in his palace, like the supports for a ship's keel, twelve of them altogether. He would stand at a great distance and let fly an arrow through them. So now I am going to set this competition to my Suitors: whichever one most easily bends the bow in his hands and shoots through all twelve axes, that is the man I shall follow, turning my back on my father's house.   (19.570 ff.)

Odysseus encourages her to proceed: she must no longer defer the competition; resourceful Odysseus will arrive,

before these men, handling this polished bow, draw
the string tight and shoot the arrow through the iron.
(19.584ff.)

Later Penelope announces the competition to the Suitors in identical words (21.67ff.); and Eurymachus says what a disgrace it would be if the Suitors should fail, whereas a vagabond beggar should

easily bend the bow and shoot through the iron.
(23.318ff.)

Meanwhile Telemachus has prepared the ground:

First he set up the axes, having dug one long trench for all of them; and he made them straight to the line and piled up[1] earth on both sides of them. And all were astonished to see how neatly he set them up; for he had never seen it done before.   (21.118ff.)

The exhibition-shot itself is described as follows:

> From the very chair, as he sat, Odysseus shot the arrow, aiming straight ahead; and he did not miss the handle-tip of all the axes, but the shaft went clear through to the door. (21.420ff.)

The question has long been debated, what is meant by 'shooting through the axes' (if indeed that is what the words signify). Professor Woodhouse, in his entertaining book, *The Composition of the Odyssey*, expressed the opinion of the majority when he wrote: 'What "shooting through the axes" really was, what the axes were like to look at, how when set up they were "like oaken stays"—all this is a mystery towards the elucidation of which neither commentators nor archaeologists have been able to contribute much of value'. It may be so; but it seems a pity if so large a part of the story is to remain for ever unintelligible. Let us inquire once more, having first briefly defined the normal meaning of certain words, in particular πέλεκυς, στειλειή, and δρύοχοι.

(1) πέλεκυς: Throughout Greek literature this word regularly denotes the whole axe, not the head as distinguished from the handle. If the context should happen to require it, we should of course allow that anybody might say 'axe' when he meant 'axe-head';[2] but we start from the position that it means the whole axe as usual.

(2) στειλειή: This noun occurs in masculine, feminine, and neuter forms.[3] In all its forms, and in all the occurrences thereof, it means the handle of an instrument as distinguished from the head. The feminine form is no exception to the rule. It occurs in three other places only. In Antiphanes fr. 121 K. the meaning is very plain, for the στειλειή, 'handle', is being contrasted with the hole in the axe-head; in Apollonius of Rhodes 4.957 we read that Hephaestus leant on the στελεὴ of his hammer—obviously on the handle[4] of it, not on the hole in the head; and in Nicander *Ther.* 386f. a snake is said to be of the thickness of the στειλειὴ[5] of a mattock—evidently again the handle, not a hole in the head. Thus the evidence of usage,

including the testimony of so good a Homerist as Apollonius, is quite unambiguous: στειλειή, like the masculine and neuter forms, means 'handle' wherever it occurs; we shall never be satisfied with any explanation of our problem which renders the word as anything but 'handle'. No question would ever have arisen here, had not some ancient commentator on the *Odyssey*, baffled as we are by the description of the exhibition-shot, proposed a solution which interprets στειλειή not as the handle but as the hole in the axe-head into which the handle is inserted. This rendering is, as we have seen, contradicted by the evidence of usage; it occurs nowhere except in comments on this problem in the *Odyssey* and their posterity.[6] If we are told that we are confronted by a 'solid phalanx' of 'all the ancient commentators and lexicographers, that is, the whole weight of Alexandrian and Graeco-Roman learning',[7] we reply that there is no solid phalanx except of parrots; no weight of learning, only a few repetitions of someone's attempt to make sense of this passage in the *Odyssey*. We are obliged to interpret στειλειή as 'handle', since there exists no evidence in the world that it was ever used by any ancient author in any other sense.[8]

(3) δρύοχοι: Telemachus set the axes up ἑξείης, δρυόχους ὥς, in a row, like the stocks on which a ship-builder lays the keel. The word is rare, but the meaning is certain enough.[9] It means 'keel-supports', blocks or cradles on which a keel is laid in the shipyard. The ancient commentators describe this common apparatus as a row of blocks or pegs or supports—ξύλα, πάσσαλοι, στηρίγματα—set level at intervals on the ground in a straight line; simple devices answering to this description may by seen on many a coast all over the world. We shall reject all solutions of our problem which do not set the axes out in a straight line spaced at intervals in such a way that they resemble some kind of stocks on which you might lay a keel.

(4) πρώτη στειλειή: This is capable of two different meanings, 'first handle', and 'handle-tip'.[10]

(5) διοϊστεῦσαι σιδήρου: Both noun and verb are ambiguous. The verb may signify either 'shoot *through*', that is, 'penetrate', or 'shoot *over*', that is, from one end of a line to the other (not

necessarily penetrating anything except the air). In Pindar *Nem.* 6.40 πέτεται διὰ θαλάσσας means 'fly in a line over the sea', not 'through the sea'; the usage is common, and in the only other Homeric context (*Od.* 12.102) the verb διοϊστεύειν plainly means 'shoot across an intervening space', not 'shoot *through*' something. As for the noun, it may be taken literally to mean 'the iron' of the axes, or more broadly 'the iron axes' as a whole.

Let us now begin with the explanation prevalent throughout antiquity. Twelve axe-heads, without handles, are to be set up

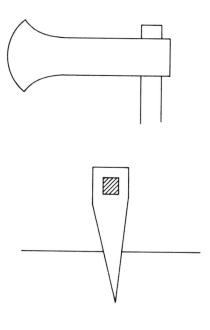

Fig. 1.

on edge in a line, with their holes facing the archer, who shoots through them as through a discontinuous tunnel (Fig. 1). This was the best that the ancient commentators could do. They must have known, as we do, that στειλειή means the handle, not the hole in the axe-head; but we should sympathize with them, if the problem were indeed solved by this device. The fact remains that the shot cannot be reconciled with the description in the text. For what sense can now be made of the words 'He did not miss the πρώτη στειλειή of all the axes'? It must mean either 'he did not miss the first hole of all the axe-heads', a sentence which it would be lenient to describe as ludicrous; or 'he did not miss the tip of the hole of all the axes', an expression which may well be judged unintelligible. There is no point whatsoever in any reference to the top of the hole, or to the bottom of the hole, of 'all twelve axes'. It has been asserted in defence of the ancients that 'the arrow would drop slightly in its trajectory, no matter how strongly it was shot, so that Odysseus must shoot as high up as possible in each hole': but nobody cares about gravitational fall over so short a distance; and if we did care, we should aim not near the top of all the holes, or indeed of the first hole, but near the bottom of the first hole, directing the arrow slightly upwards through the tunnel. And I ask whether anybody seriously believes that such an aim could be described in these words, 'he did not miss the tip of the hole of all twelve axes'. The hard fact is that the adjective πρώτη is never going to make any sense so long as στειλειή is taken to mean 'hole in the axe-head'. If it means 'handle', πρώτη στειλειή may very well mean 'handle-tip'; but before we follow that guiding light, let us briefly contemplate another illusion, created (I believe) by the Comte de Caylus in 1781,[11] cherished by A. S. Murray a century later, and revered as the true light by Helbig, Monro, Butcher and Lang, and A. D. Fraser.[12]

We are to imagine axes with ready-made holes in the blades, or with heads forming a loop on one side, like that of the Amazon on the archaic metope at Selinus (Fig. 2). Odysseus is to shoot through the loops of twelve such axes in a line. I linger

Fig. 2.

only a moment in this now desolate region. A line of these abnormal axes could not have suggested the comparison to a row of keel-stocks; nor could the shooting of an arrow through such openings have been described by the words 'he did not miss the $\pi\rho\dot{\omega}\tau\eta$ $\sigma\tau\epsilon\iota\lambda\epsilon\iota\dot{\eta}$ of all the axes'. Once more, both the adjective $\pi\rho\dot{\omega}\tau\eta$ and the noun $\sigma\tau\epsilon\iota\lambda\epsilon\iota\dot{\eta}$ have become not so much superfluous as downright meaningless.

An entirely different approach was made by A. Goebel in 1876.[13] He rightly insisted that $\sigma\tau\epsilon\iota\lambda\epsilon\iota\dot{\eta}$ means 'handle', not 'hole', and he suggested a shot through the tunnel formed by a

FIG. 3.

line of recurved axe-heads of a type known (by us, not at that time by Goebel) to be characteristic of Minoan Crete (Fig. 3). It is obvious that if no more than this is meant, that the arrow passed between the blades, we should still be leaving the words πρώτης στειλειῆς unexplained; let us therefore look at them again more closely. The poet said 'πελέκεων οὐκ ἤμβροτε πάντων / πρώτης στειλειῆς': there are two ways of analyzing the grammar, the way of reason and the way of chaos. Choosing the way of chaos, we take πελέκεων as directly governed by οὐκ ἤμβροτε, 'he did not miss the axes', and then wonder in vain what account can be given of the genitive case in πρώτης στειλειῆς. I have heard it called a 'genitive absolute', a grandiose way of concealing the gloomy truth that it satisfies neither sense nor syntax. I have seen it translated '*starting from the first handle*', a rendering which would enrich the language with a new idiom. Apart from the chaotic grammar, if πρώτης στειλειῆς is to be thus elbowed out the way, what need was there for any mention of 'handles' or 'handle-tips' at all? The arrow might be said to start from the first axe (though we were in no danger of thinking that it might have started from the second or third); but why tell us that it started from the first *handle*? The ὕβρις of arbitrary grammar has reaped the ἄτη of miserable sense. This word for 'handle' (of whatever gender) is rare in literature; the handle of an axe is something which you do not specially distinguish (particularly when, as here, the axe is not being taken in hand) unless there is a motive: what is the motive here?

The correct way, indeed the only possible way, is to take πρώτης στειλειῆς as the direct object of οὐκ ἤμβροτε, making the genitive case of πελέκεων depend on στειλειῆς, 'handle of the axes'. What is actually said, therefore, is that Odysseus 'did not miss the handle-tip of all the axes'; and we shall not acquiesce in any explanation which leaves the handle-tip of any of the twelve axes untouched. It was clearly necessary for Goebel to take a further step; and indeed he took it, though heavy of heart: the arrow, he said, must actually have brushed the top surfaces of all the handles as it passed down the line of axe-blades.[14]

Goebel's argument is lucid and logical. His conclusion is unavoidable; and it is also plainly unacceptable. The motif is intrinsically improbable: it is a far-fetched and over-subtle notion, that an ordeal by bow and arrow should consist in this—shooting so as to graze the top surfaces of a line of axe-handles. Moreover it is a commonplace in tales of this kind that the act must not only be performed, it must also be seen to have been performed. Let one of the Suitors exclaim 'Missed the lot by half a millimetre!' and we are confounded; we

cannot possibly refute him. You could watch the arrow, however strongly shot; but you could not observe whether it just
had or just had not brushed the surface of the handles. I used
to think that if Goebel was right there must be something
missing from the description—that Odysseus must have shot
an arrow which brushed the surfaces of the handles as it passed
down the line *and tipped each axe over to the ground*. A pretty
shot, most pleasing and picturesque; but, if the fact was so,
why was it not stated? We should have to argue (not un-
reasonably) that the poet is describing a traditional feat which
he did not fully understand.

We reject the axe-head theory of the ancients, the loop and
handle-tip theories of the moderns; are we at the end of our
tether? On the contrary, the best is yet to be. Before we come
to it, consider an ingenious and novel interpretation, lurking
unnoticed or despised, *obiter dictum* in a dozen words by Van
Leeuwen in his edition of the *Odyssey*:[15] *ergone summa capita
duodecim bipennium in aula erectarum heros sagitta perforavit?*—
the arrow penetrated and passed clean through the handle-tips
of all twelve axes.

The world has almost wholly ignored this; and the world is
wrong. Despite the apparent objections which leap so nimbly
to our minds, this is a better solution than any hitherto considered; and it has certain merits unnoticed by its author. It
leaves nothing in the text unexplained, and it really is a very
pretty shot. Among our first objections may be the allegation
that the shot is impossible; and I shall now say a word on this
topic, in relation both to Goebel's brushing of handle-tips,
which requires absolute straightness of line, and to Van
Leeuwen's penetration-shot, which demands stupendous
strength in the archer.

Let it be frankly admitted that whereas the Goebel-shot is
at least theoretically possible, the Van Leeuwen–shot can have
no other home than fairytale or folklore. The Goebel-shot is
possible on two assumptions: that there is no gravitational fall
over the short distance; and that it is possible for an arrow to
skim over such surfaces without deflection. It is likely that both

assumptions would be tacitly made by the Homeric audience. The feat is little (if at all) beyond what is possible with an arrow shot from a heavy bow over a very short distance; and what we need here is a truly wonderful shot beyond the capacity of all except the hero. We are not interested in gravitational fall or deflection; we do not care whether the shot is in fact just possible or just not possible for an exceptionally strong and skilful archer.

Tales of marvellously accurate archery are beloved of all ages and sorts of men—except the champion archer, who knows what nonsense most of them are. The English champion C. J. Longman,[16] who collected and examined reports from all over the world, writes that 'the feats which have been accredited to the American Indians, and many other races, would be marvellous if performed by men armed with the finest modern small-bore rifles aided by range-finders, telescopes, and windgauges'. Gordon Grimley[17] reminded us in 1958 that at the Olympic Games early in this century the elect native archers of Africa, Japan, the Americas, and elsewhere, faced with a target four feet by six feet at forty-two yards range, recorded only two hits. Californian Indians, who had lived by the bow, when tested in 1911, more often missed than hit a four-feet-square target at forty yards.[18] Nevertheless the expert target-archer has been known to attain an accuracy of the sort we are looking for. I say nothing of William Tell, for his achievement was eclipsed in 1955 by François Perréard, who 'repeatedly shot an apple off the top of his eight-year-old son's head at 25 metres'[19]—that was a truly marvellous, and very dangerous, exercise; of which camera-films may (or might then) be seen. And we must reckon that what matters is not the truth but what people will readily believe: listen to this, for example—'In the reign of Henry IV, in shooting-matches, 300 yards was the common target, and the ordinary mark was a straight willow hazel-rod, as thick as a man's thumb, and 5 feet in length; and such a mark as this a really good archer held it shame to miss'. That is nonsense; but it is not quoted from travelers' tales or medieval gossip. It stands in the *New*

American Cyclopedia, 1861, under the title *Archery*. If such stuff can be believed by a modern author and printed by sober encyclopedists for the misleading of you and me, let us not listen to any complaint that the accuracy of the Goebel-shot would have strained the credulity of its audience. Suffice it to say that three hundred yards, here called 'the common range', was about the extreme limit of distance (no question of aiming) for the greatest of nineteenth-century archers, Mr. H. A. Ford;[20] as for that hazel-rod 'an inch or so broad', you might as well tell a modern golfer that in former days men 'held it shame' to take more than one stroke a hole.[21]

Goebel is credible; not so Van Leeuwen. No audience familiar with archery would believe for one moment that an arrow could penetrate twelve pieces of wood in succession. If you choose your wood soft enough and your bow heavy enough you can indeed shoot clean through a board an inch thick. Dr. Saxton Pope[22] made some experiments and reported in 1925 that in 'shooting a blunt arrow from a 75-pound bow at a white-pine board an inch thick, the shaft will often go completely through it'. But let the wood be anything but soft, and the strongest shot will do no more than pierce it, so that the point emerges on the other side. One very seldom quotes an English king in a paper on Homer: there survives a manuscript note by Edward IV, dated 14 May 1450, recording an experiment made by archers of his Guard—'they shot at an inch-board, which some pierced quite';[23] the board was of 'well-seasoned timber', but there is no telling whether 'pierced quite' means 'passed clean through' or merely penetrated in the more limited sense. We must allow for the same ambiguity when Giraldus Cambrensis tells us that Welsh bowmen once penetrated a portal of oak *palmaris fere spissitudinis*.[24] I think we must admit that the Homeric audience would readily accept the passing through a single axe-handle; they would know that it would not penetrate a second, and twelve successive penetrations would appear to them much more unrealistic than tales about one-eyed giants or men turned into swine. You could not be quite sure that there never was a Circe or a Cyclops, but you knew from your own experience that the penetration of twelve axe-handles by a single arrow was a physical impossibility.

This is by no means a fatal objection to Van Leeuwen's theory; and I have not yet mentioned the greatest of his virtues. For is it not true that a penetration shot of this general type is a traditional feature of this legend at large? Here is an obvious question to ask; yet, until recently, only one man (so far as I know) had ever answered it; and he, not being primarily a classical scholar, went his way unlistened to. It is certain that some of the tales told in the *Odyssey* recur, in more or less the same form, in universal folklore; and some of the Odyssean tales become first intelligible in the light of fuller versions to be found elsewhere. What then of the Arrow and the Axes? The Odyssean account is obscure and elliptic, all men agree; let it then be asked, are there other versions of this motif, such that we can supply from them the links missing in the *Odyssey*?

Extraordinary feats with bow and arrow are common enough in saga and fairytale and what passes for history; but this particular motif—the shooting of an arrow through a series of objects as a test of skill or a proof of identity or otherwise to win a woman—seems to be very rare. I see no example in Aarne-Thompson's *Types of the Folk-Tale* or in Stith Thompson's *Motif-Index of Folk-Literature*. There is indeed almost no firm ground anywhere except on the path pioneered by W. Crooke[25] in 1908 and broadly paved by Gabriel Germain[26] in 1954. Crooke drew attention to the fact that the only close parallels to the Odyssean episode are to be found in tales from India:

First, the story of Rasālu,[27] in which certain 'giants brought out the seven (iron) griddles, each of which weighed 35 tons, and setting them up in a row one behind another they challenged Rasālu to pierce them'; we guess that he will, and he does.

Second, a passage from the Pāli book *The Jātaka*,[28] wherein the hero pierces 'a hundred boards joined together'.

It is Crooke's third example, to be conjoined with a fourth, which strikes a familiar note and compels our close attention. This motif, the piercing of objects in succession with an arrow, in order to establish a claim to a woman's hand—a motif extremely rare in universal folklore—recurs in both the old Sanskrit epics, the *Mahābhārata* and (with one modification) the *Rāmāyana*.

In the former the king's daughter is won by Prince Arjuna; like Odysseus, he is in disguise; like Odysseus, he bends a bow unbendable by others; like Odysseus, he performs a wonderful exhibition-shot. A target is fixed, and a disk pierced by five holes is set revolving in front of it; Arjuna must shoot five arrows, one through each of the holes in the disk as it revolves in front of the target:

> To the helmed son of Pandu, Arjun, pride of Kuru's race,
> Drupad longed to give his daughter, peerless in her maiden grace,
> And of massive wood unbending Drupad made a stubborn bow;
> Saving Arjun, prince or chieftain might not bend the weapon low;
> And he made a whirling discus, hung it 'neath the open sky,
> And beyond the whirling discus placed a target far and high.
> 'Whoso strings this bow', said Drupad, 'hits the target in his pride,
> Through the high and circling discus, he shall win Panchala's bride'.

. . .

> Godlike Arjun, born of Indra, filled with Vishnu's matchless might,
> Bent the wondrous bow of Drupad, fixed the shining darts aright,
> Through the disc the shining arrows fly with strange and hissing sound,
> Hit and pierce the distant target, bring it thundering on the ground.[29]

In the *Rāmāyana* the king promises his daughter Sita to the man who can bend and string a massive bow (5,000 men were needed to bring it on the scene). Rāma bends it, strings it—and then deliberately breaks it in two: in this story, the exhibition-shot has been transferred from this courtship-ordeal to a different context: Sugrīva asks Rāma for protection against his brother Valin; prepares a line of seven trees in the forest; and requires Rāma to prove his quality by shooting an arrow clean through the tree-stems. Rāma 'took his formidable bow and an arrow, full of pride' and

> To prove his might, his arrows through
> Seven palms in line uninjured flew.[30]

Nobody can read the stories of Arjuna and Rāma without noticing the close similarity in outline and in detail to the Odyssean episode. The courtship of the lady; the disguise of the prince; the bending of the bow; the miraculous exhibition-shot—these and other features were evidently common to the old Greek and to the old Indian epics; they are very seldom attested elsewhere.[31] It is obviously probable that the two streams have a common source—that the whole story of the bride-winning by bow-ordeal originated in that remote period when the Indo-Europeans were a more or less undifferentiated people; and that it became the common heritage of both Indian and European branches of the family. In the *Odyssey*, as in the Indian epics, we read the latest version of a tale which had been told in the steppe-lands of central Asia a millennium and a half before the time of Homer.[32]

The ordeal of Rāma, whose arrow 'through seven palms in line uninjured flew', compels us to take seriously the suggestion of Van Leeuwen, that Odysseus' arrow actually penetrated the twelve axe-handles in succession. The story is essentially the same in both versions; and there is no significant difference between shooting through seven trees and shooting through twelve upright axe-handles. Agreed, the feat is impossible—for that very reason, perhaps, it is not precisely described in the *Odyssey*; the last word, which would have proved a bowshot of supernatural strength, has not been spoken. If I am still dissatisfied, it is mainly because there is a single fundamental question which is still left unanswered, indeed unasked: why *axes*? If you are to shoot through twelve wooden objects in a line, why choose (of all things) axe-handles? To this I add a second rather frivolous-sounding question, which may nevertheless prove helpful—what are twelve axes doing in the palace anyway? If we could give an explanation which answered these questions and all the other questions too, we shall have done as well as we shall ever do.

We asked at the beginning what πέλεκυς means, and answered, 'an axe'. That answer seemed safe enough; on reflection we see that it was seriously misleading. An axe, according to Webster's Dictionary, is 'a cutting tool . . . it consists of an edged head fixed to a handle'. Very well; but the Greek word πέλεκυς means both this and something very different—not only a cutting-tool but also a cult-object. In Minoan and Mycenaean palaces axes were hung on walls, perched between bulls' horns, stuck into pillars. And shrines of the Geometric period tell a similar tale; miniature bronze and iron axes, offerings of piety, have been found in the temples of Hera at Olympia, of Ortheia at Sparta, of Artemis at Lousoi in Arcadia; in Delphi, in Cyprus, and elsewhere[33] (Fig. 4). Whether the Odyssean shot is an heirloom from the remotest past (as we believe) or an invention of the Ionian epic, the audience will think it very natural that the royal palace should be well equipped with these cult-objects; and they will know, what we have waited long to learn, that there is one great difference between the household-axe and the cult-axe—a difference which explains why axes should be selected to compose a target for the exhibition-shot.

So far as I know, no household-axe or battle-axe has survived with handle intact; naturally, since the handle was made of perishable material. But there are many pictures of such axes in Black-Figure and Red-Figure painting, especially in scenes of the birth of Athena.[34] In all that I have seen, the axe consists of a head and a handle, and there is nothing peculiar about the

Artemis: Lousoi
(*Oest. Jahreshefte IV*
1901, p. 49, fig. 67).

Delphi
(*Fouilles de Delphes, V*
1908, p. 210, fig. 444).

Ortheia: Sparta
(*Artemis Orthia* 1929, p. 199, plate LXXXV K).

FIG. 4.

handle. It is quite otherwise with the cult-axe. Few of these have survived with the handle intact for the whole of its length; but of these few quite a high proportion have a most pleasing peculiarity. The base of the handle is pierced, and often enough rounded into a ring, for suspension. Fig. 5 shows an example from a Geometric Boeotian sherd,[35] a votive axe, hanging on the wall. Stand twelve such axes in a line upside down (the usual posture for cult-axes hanging on the wall),

FIG. 5. Votive axe on wall: Boeotian Geometric sherd
(Blinkenberg, *Arch. Stud.*, 1904, p. 46, fig. 28.)

and Odysseus will have a target which leaves nothing in the
text unexplained; moreover we shall understand why axes—
these, and no other objects—were chosen for the target: the
heads make a firm base; the rings make a challenging target;
and just these suitable objects, cult-axes, are sure to be abun-
dant in the royal palace. The resemblance of the bases to
keel-stocks is obvious enough (Fig. 6); and the description 'did
not miss the handle-tips of all twelve axes' is now for the first
time wholly intelligible. The man who shoots through the
handle-tips of all the axes is the one man whose action can be
properly so described; he may also be said to shoot 'through
the iron', for the cult-axe (unlike the household-axe) is nor-
mally made of bronze or iron wholly, the handle as well as the
head. The arrow which passes through the handle-holes is
indeed passing *through the iron*.

And let there be no complaint about impossibility. The
Homeric audience will be satisfied with a shot of extreme

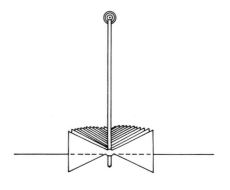

Fig. 6.

difficulty and delicacy; it will care nothing for gravitational
fall; it will perhaps be offended by a gross and patent impossibility, but there is no such question here. Suppose the
twelve axes placed at yard intervals, and suppose the holes to
be only a little greater in diameter than the arrow-shaft: the
shot is then technically possible at the limit of a Circus Strong-
Man's power. If you could string a hundred-pound bow, you
could probably shoot in a straight line for a dozen yards. I must
add, on the authority of a champion archer, that such a shot
'would indicate marvellously strong shooting', even if the
rings were as much as four inches in diameter and the distance
only twelve yards.[36] But 'marvellously strong shooting' is just
what we are looking for; it would never occur to us to calculate

diameters or any other dimensions; we would go so far as to allow that the holes may be only just large enough to admit the passage of the arrow; but the truth is that we do not concern ourselves with that or any other such detail.

There would be no doubt that the feat had actually been performed. Even at the speed required, it would be possible to distinguish whether the arrow had passed through the holes or outside them; though I have little doubt that in an earlier version, as in the *Mahābhārata*, a target was fixed in line with the holes, to be hit only by an arrow which had passed through the holes.[37]

Finally, a word about the past history of this explanation. Carl Schuchhardt[38] recommended it, briefly and without discussion or proof, in 1935. He did not refer to C. Blinkenberg,[39] who had said the same thing thirty-one years earlier, with some but still by no means adequate argument. Blinkenberg's explanation has a long history in England: it is the version adopted by Pope in his translation of the *Odyssey*:

> The whizzing arrow vanish'd from the string,
> Sung on direct, and threaded every ring.

The accompanying illustration[40] shows Odysseus about to shoot through a series of rings on the butts of axe-handles whose heads are buried in the ground. No doubt it would be possible (I have not tried) to trace the explanation much further back; and indeed there is good reason to believe that it was current in remote antiquity: *The Etymologicum Magnum* s.v. δρύοχοι has an entry concerned with Odysseus' exhibition-shot: 'Some understand large rings attached to uprights fixed in the ground, to shoot through';[41] surely an explanation very similar to that which I have given.[42]

Notes

I. The Lotus-Eaters

1. In the notes to this chapter 'Radermacher' = L. Radermacher, *Die Erzählungen der Odyssee: Sitzungsberichte der Kais. Akad. der Wissenschaften in Wien, Phil.-Hist. Klasse*, 178 (1916) 1ff.; 'Lamer' = *RE* 13 (1927) 1507ff., *s.v.* 'Lotophagen'; 'Steier' = *RE* 13 (1927) 1515ff., *s.v.* 'Lotos'; Goodyear = W. H. Goodyear, *The Grammar of the Lotus* (London 1891).

2. I should prefer to shirk the task of defining precisely what I mean by 'folktale'. See Aly, *RE* 14 (1928) 254f.; G. S. Kirk, *Myth: Its Meaning and Functions in Ancient and Other Cultures* (Cambridge 1970) 31f. The question is complex, especially in the *Odyssey*, where the distinction between folktale and saga is deliberately blurred. A broad and obvious line may be drawn between a species of 'folktale', as concerned with creatures of grotesque form and supernatural powers, living in an imaginary world, and a species of 'saga', as concerned with persons believed to be historical and represented as behaving realistically in the actual world. Although the distinction is blurred in the Homeric poems, it is not obliterated: the difference between Hecuba and Circe or between Ajax and Polyphemus is the difference, or rather an aspect of the difference, between saga and folktale; in *Od.* 9–12 the blurring of the line of demarcation is more thorough than in the rest of the poem.

3. See Radermacher 47, n. 1, 48, n. 2; W. Spletstösser, *Der heimkehrende Gatte und sein Weib in der Weltliteratur* (Berlin 1899). Lesky, *Homeros* (*RE* Suppl. 11, 1967) 115f.; Crooke, *Folk-Lore* 19 (1908) 154f.; my *Homeric Odyssey* 18, n. 1; S. Trenkner, *The Greek Novella in the Classical Period* (Cambridge 1958) 61.

4. Hom. *Il.* 2.846.

5. Γέρμαρα· Κελτικῆς ἔθνος ὃ τὴν ἡμέραν οὐ βλέπει· ὡς Ἀριστοτέλης περὶ θαυμασίων, τοὺς δὲ Λωτοφάγους καθεύδειν ἐξάμηνον.

6. Xenophon, *Anab.* 3.2.25; Plato, *Rep.* 8.560C; Plut. *repugn. Stoic.* 2; Max. Tyr. 20.4; Lucian, *Nigr.* 3.38, *merc. cond.* 8, *salt.* 8; three or four references in Libanius; Palladas *Anth. Pal.* 9.284; Cic. *Fam.* 7.20; Prop. 3.12.17; Ovid. *Remed.* 789, *ex Ponto* 4.10.18; *Culex* 124; *Paneg. Messall.* 55; Silius Ital. 3.310; Ammianus 14.6.21. Most of these are very brief allusions (ὥσπερ οἱ Λωτοφάγοι; *ut Homerici bacarum suavitate Lotophagi*), and doubtless a few more of this type

could be assembled. The proverbial nature of reference to the Λωτοφάγοι is recognized in Apostol. 11.2. *Cf.* Jessen, *Myth. Lex.* 2.2142f.

7. Hyginus, *Fab.* 125.

8. Herodotus 4.176f.

9. Ibid. 4.180.

10. The references are assembled and discussed by Lamer, 1507ff., and Jessen, *Myth. Lex.* 2.2143.

11. Herodotus 4.184, 191–192.

12. L. G. Pocock, *Reality and Allegory in the Odyssey* (Amsterdam 1959) 53.

13. See Lamer 1571–1574; Radermacher 10f.; Lesky, *Homeros* 113.

14. As Sir William Thiselton-Dyer said, 'λωτός is a name applied to a number of widely different plants, but the idea of edibility seems to underlie them all' (*Companion to Greek Studies*[2] [1931] 60). In Homer, apart from this context and the summary of it in *Od.* 23.311, reference to λωτός is rare. It is plainly 'clover' in *Il.* 21.351 (named together with θρύον and κύπειρον) and 2.776 (horse-fodder = *Hymn. Herm.* 107; the force of formula-tradition has induced the poet to apply the phrase λωτὸν ἐρεπτόμενοι to his Lotus-Eaters, the verb being proper to animals) and *Od.* 4.603 (coupled with κύπειρον). In *Il.* 14.347 it is presumably 'lotus' or at least some kind of lily, fit company for 'crocus' and 'hyacinth'; and so I suppose in *Il.* 12.283, πεδία λωτεῦντα.

15. For detail, see Lamer 1511f.

16. I am much indebted to Steier, whose essay on the lotus is notably well informed, and to Goodyear. The Royal Horticultural Society's *Dictionary of Gardening* (1956) keeps the layman to a straight and narrow path for *Nelumbo* (p. 1359), *Nymphaea* (p. 1387), and *Zizyphus* (p. 2311).

17. There is an excellent illustration of *Nelumbo* in Goodyear p. 30, fig. 10.

18. It is generally supposed that Hymn 4.34.5 in the *Atharva-veda* ('the oval-fruited lotus spreads his fibre . . .') refers to the edible lotus. Cf. A. A. Macdonell in *The Encyclopaedia of Religion and Ethics* VIII (1915) 142f.; R. T. H. Griffith, *The Hymns of the Atharva-Veda* (Benares 1895) 1.177.

19. Macdonell 142f.; J. Campbell, *The Masks of God*, vol. II, *Oriental Mythology*, 486f.; A. Daniélou, *Hindu Polytheism* (London 1964) 156.

20. Goodyear 11, n. 47; cf. *The Jātaka, or Stories of the Buddha's Former Births, Translated from the Pāli by Various Hands under the Editorship of Professor E. B. Cowell*, I (Cambridge 1895) 1.41. Plate X in *The Mythology of All Races*, ed. L. H. Gray and G. F. Moore (Boston 1916–1932) 6.120, shows Brahma being born, emerging from a lotus which springs from the navel of Vishnu.

21. Goodyear 31f.

22. *Jātaka* 1.4, 14.488.

23. Especially in China. Goodyear (p. 34) says that *Nelumbo* was first introduced to America by Mr. E. D. Sturtevant about 1876 at Bordentown, New Jersey. A single plant proliferated to cover three-quarters of an acre in eight years; 'the boys of the neighbourhood discovered the edible properties of the filbert-like seed, and made their nutting excursions to the new source of supplies'. This lotus soon became a staple food of the American Indians.

24. W. M. Flinders Petrie, *The Encyclopedia of Religion and Ethics* VIII (1915) 140f.; Wallis Budge, *The Gods of the Egyptians* (1904) 1.520f.; Steier 1522; Goodyear 3f.

25. Herodotus 2.92. It looks as though Hipponax mentioned the root of this lotus in his Odyssean poem, fr. 77 (Masson).

26. Goodyear says 'like a watering-pot'; the illustration (p. 30) shows an object very like the rose of a watering-can.

27. Theophrastus *HP* 4.8.9.

28. Steier 1524.

29. Steier 1515; Boisacq, *Dict. Étym.* 595. H. Frisk, *Gr. Etym. Wörterbuch* 2 (1970) 153, is doubtful: 'Mittelmeerwort unsicheren Ursprungs, nach Lewy *Fremdw.* 46 mit Muss-Arnolt aus hebr. *lōṭ*'.

30. *Hymn Demet.* 370ff.

31. If that really is what ἀμφὶ ἑ νωμήσας means; I doubt it, but have no likelier suggestion.

32. From E. B. Tylor, *Primitive Culture* (London, 3rd ed. 1891) 2.51.

33. From David Leslie, *Among the Zulus and Amatongas* (Edinburgh, 2nd ed. 1875) 121.

34. From Richard Taylor, *Te ika a Maui, or, New Zealand and Its Inhabitants* (London, 2nd ed. 1870) 271.

35. From *Folk-Lore* 10 (1899) 300.

36. From R. H. Codrington, *The Melanesians: Studies in Their Anthropology and Folk-Lore* (Oxford 1891) 277.

37. Lamer 1514.

38. From John Rhys, *Celtic Folklore: Welsh and Manx* (Oxford 1901) 1.290.

39. From Mary Frere, *Hindoo Fairy Legends* (*Old Deccan Days*), (New York 1967; a reprint of the 3rd ed. of *Old Deccan Days*, 1881).

40. From O. L. Jiriczek, *Faeröische Märchen und Sagen*, in *Zeitschr. d. Vereins für Volkskunde* 2.1892.2; Radermacher 11.

41. *Kalevala* 16.293.

42. Saxo Grammaticus 8.288ff. (p.449 Jantzen): (' wer nämlich von jenen Speisen koste, verliere die Erinnerung an alles'); Radermacher 11.

43. Sufficient references will be found in Radermacher 10f.; Allen, Halliday, and Sikes, *The Homeric Hymns* (1936) 169; E. S. Hartland, *The Science of Fairy Tales* (Methuen, 2nd ed. 1925) 38ff. Hartland notes (p. 47) that the motif is as widely applied in fairyland contexts as in underworld contexts.

44. Radermacher, *passim*.

II. The Laestrygonians

1. Pfuhl, *Malerei und Zeichnung der Griechen* 2.883, 890ff., with references there and in Meuli, *RE* Suppl. 5 (1931) 540; cf. Höfer in *Myth. Lex.* 2.1807; Fr. Müller, *Odyssee-Illustrationen* 145f.; excellent colour reproductions in K. Woermann, *Die antiken Odyssee-Landschaften vom Esquilinischen Hügel zu Rom* (Munich 1876).

2. Lycophron 956f.

3. *Metam.* 14.233ff.

4. *Ibis* 390.

5. Juvenal 15.18.

6. Hor. *carm.* 3.16.34, *Laestrygonia amphora*; Statius *Silv.* 1.3.84; Silius Ital. 7.276, 410, 8.531, 14.125f.

7. Thuc. 6.2.1.

8. Hesiod, fr. 150.25f. M.-W., *Αἴτν]ην παιπαλόεσσαν* ... *'Ο]ρτυγίην Λαιστ[ρ]υ[γον]ίην τε γενέθλην.*

9. Theopompus *ap.* Polyb. 8.11.13, *Λαιστρυγόνας τοὺς τὸ Λεοντῖνον πεδίον οἰκήσαντας*; Strabo 1.2.9; Pliny, *NH* 3.8.14, 49; Hesych. *s.v.*; Steph. Byz. *s.v.*; Schol. Hom. *Od.* 10.86.

10. Hor. *carm.* 3.16.34; Pliny, *NH* 3.5.9, 59; Statius, *Silv.* 1.3.84; Silius Ital. 7.276, 410, 8.531.

11. My *Homeric Odyssey* 18; especially O. Hackman, *Die Poly-*

phemsage in der Volksüberlieferung (Akademische Abhandlung, Helsing-fors 1904).

12. See L. Frobenius, *Das Zeitalter des Sonnengottes* (Berlin 1904) 369f.; S. Trenkner, *The Greek Novella in the Classical Period* (Cambridge 1958) 51f.

13. Frobenius 376f.; L. Radermacher, *Die Erzählungen der Odyssee: Sitzungsberichte der Kais. Akad. der Wissenschaften in Wien, Phil.-Hist. Klasse*, 178 (1916) 17. Of all Frobenius' examples, this one is much the closest to the Homeric version.

14. H. J. Rose, *Greek Mythology* (1928) 14. The Laestrygonians, like Grendel in *Beowulf*, are credible in all things except size; see Gilbert Highet, *The Classical Tradition* (Oxford 1949) 23.

15. See L. Radermacher, *Rhein. Mus.* 60 (1905) 588f., *Erzählungen* 17.

16. Schol. Hom. *Od.* 10.82. W. W. Merry, in his smaller edition of the *Odyssey* (note on 10.82), suggests that τηλ- in τηλέπυλος and τηλύγετος is the root seen in τηλεθάω, and signifies 'grown', i.e., 'large'. I doubt if this idea really suits either -πυλος or -μαχος.

17. See K. Meuli, *Odyssee und Argonautika* (Basel 1921); my *Homeric Odyssey* 2; A. Kirchhoff, *Die Homerische Odyssee* (Berlin 1879) 287f.

18. Hom. *Od.* 12.70.

19. F. Gisinger, *RE* Suppl. 4 (1924) 534, with literature; K. Meuli, *RE* Suppl. 5 (1931) 538f.; W. W. Merry and J. Riddell, *Homer's Odyssey*, note on 10.82; H. Vos, *Mnemosyne* 16 (1963) 18f., with recent literature.

20. It is not necessary to debate whether ἐγγύς in *Od.* 10.86 should be referred to time rather than space. Both ideas may be combined in the same adverb, as in Latin *prope*; and the distinction between time and space may be fine-drawn in Greek (Hom. *Il.* 10.251, ἐγγύθι δ᾽ ἠώς; Sappho fr. 43.9, ἄγχι γὰρ ἁμέρα; Xen. *Cyr.* 2.3.2, ἐγγὺς ἡμῖν ὁ ἀγών).

21. In *Od.* 10.191, exceptionally, the sun sets ὑπὸ γαῖαν.

22. ἆσσον ἰοῦσαι, with variant ἀμφὶς ἐοῦσαι; see M. L. West *ad loc.* Attempts to find a tolerable sense for ἀμφὶς ἐοῦσαι in this context seem to me to have failed wholly. I believe that the variant is an interpolation, an attempt to substitute something (however feeble) for a phrase which was and is hard to understand; it really is very odd to say that Night begins where Day ends, in the west. Parmenides (1.11f.) tells of a 'lintel and stone threshold'

which 'keep Night and Day apart', ἔνθα πύλαι Νυκτός τε καὶ Ἤματός εἰσι κελεύθων, / καί σφας ὑπέρθυρον ἀμφὶς ἔχει καὶ λάινος οὐδός. Here plainly, as in Hesiod, Night and Day share the same dwelling; they are 'kept apart by the threshold', in the sense that when the one is at home the other is out; they are never on the same side of the threshold at the same time. The interpolation of ἀμφὶς ἐοῦσαι in Hesiod may have been inspired by this passage of Parmenides; it does not, however, suit the context in Hesiod.

23. Mimnermus fr. 10 (Diehl); Stesichorus *PMG* fr. 185; see Kirk and Raven, *The Presocratic Philosophers* (Cambridge 1957) 14f.

24. Tac. *Agric.* 12.

25. Lehmann-Haupt, *RE* 11 (1921) 425f.

26. I have considered, but rejected, the theory of H. Vos (n. 19 above; cf. L. Woodbury, *TAPA* 97 [1966] 611f.): Where αἰθήρ prevails, there is pure and perpetual light. The dome of αἰθήρ covers the circular disc of earth, extending down to its rims. The Laestrygonians live on the edge of the disc *in der Nähe des von Licht erfüllten Aithers* (Vos 25). They therefore enjoy perpetual light. But what then can possibly be meant by saying that 'the paths (or courses; *Bahnen* is Vos's word) of Night and Day are near'? Vos rightly says (20f.) that ἐγγύς ought to mean 'near the Laestrygonians', not 'near each other'; but though it ought, it cannot, for it would make no sense. In Vos's view, what is 'near the Laestrygonians' is αἰθήρ, not the courses of Night and Day. If you need to say 'because they live near the αἰθήρ', how can you hope to be understood when what you actually say is 'because they live near *the paths of Night and Day*'? Vos's own explanation of this crucial point is plainly unacceptable: 'der Aither wird in diesem Falle "die Bahnen von Nacht und Tag" genannt, weil die Laestrygonen im Osten wohnen, wo die Sonne, der Tag und die Nacht ihre Bahn anfangen'; the 'beginning', essential to Vos's theory, is not in the text, and indeed is virtually excluded by the word which is in the text, κέλευθοι, 'the paths they follow', their track as opposed to their terminus.

The poet is explaining how a man could do a double shift of daylight-work in twenty-four hours: his explanation is to be that the man lives in the perpetual light of the αἰθήρ; and we are asked to believe that this is what he means when he says 'because the man lives near the paths followed by Night and Day'.

27. Schol. Hom. *Od.* 10.86: Κράτης βραχείας αὐτοῦ ὑποτίθεται τὰς νύκτας. καὶ γάρ φησιν αὐτοὺς εἶναι περὶ τὴν κεφαλὴν τοῦ

Δράκοντος, περὶ ἧς ῎Αρατός φησι· κείνη που κεφαλὴ τῆι νίσσεται,
ἧιχί περ ἄκραι / μίσγονται δύσιές τε καὶ ἀντολαὶ ἀλλήλησιν· ὅθεν
σύνεγγυς οὐσῶν τῶν ἀνατολῶν ταῖς δύσεσι λέγειν τὸν ποιητήν,
ἐγγὺς γὰρ νυκτός τε καὶ τὰ ἑξῆς, παρὰ τὸ πλησιάζειν τὰς τῆς
νυκτὸς κελεύθους ταῖς τοῦ ἥματος κελεύθοις ἢ τὴν νύκτα ἐγγὺς
τετάχθαι τῆς ἡμέρας βραχυτάτην οὖσαν.

28. Quoted from G. R. Mair on Aratus (Loeb edition) 61f.

29. See Blümner, *RE* 3 (1897) 295f.

30. *Ibid*. 300.

31. H. L. Lorimer, *Homer and the Monuments* (1950) 16, 25; for Minoan Crete, Evans, *PM* 2.174.

32. ἤλεκτρον is 'amber' in *Od*. 15.460, χρύσεον ὅρμον ἔχων, μετὰ δ' ἠλέκτροισιν ἔερτο, *Od*. 18.295f. ὅρμον . . . χρύσεον, ἠλέκτροισιν ἐερμένον, but presumably not in *Od*. 4.73, χρυσοῦ τ' ἠλέκτρου τε καὶ ἀργύρου ἠδ 'ἐλέφαντος. The word does not occur in the *Iliad*.

33. Blümner 301f.

34. Blümner 297f.

35. Anderson on Tac. *Agric.* p. 74; mark especially the antiquated pseudo-scientific nonsense of *Agric.* 13.4 (*scilicet extrema . . .*).

36. Caesar *BG* 5.13.

37. Translated by Petis de la Croix (Paris 1722) 3.13.

38. Gibbon, *History of the Decline and Fall of the Roman Empire* ch. 65.

39. Pliny *NH* 2.77, 4.30. Hipparchus would be specially interesting, if only we had a less muddled representative of his writing than Strabo, 2.1.18f.

40. There is a large literature on Pytheas; a good introduction, and sober judgment, in W. W. Hyde, *Ancient Greek Mariners* (1947) 124f.

41. J. D. P. Bolton, *Aristeas of Proconnesus* (1962) 187, writes 'it may be that Laestrygonia is a purely imaginary country enjoying a perpetual twilight'. I am sure that it was a purely imaginary country, but still it had a location, however ill-defined—it was on our earth, in a particular quarter of it. And what it enjoyed, according to Homer, was not perpetual twilight but almost perpetual daylight.

III. Circe

1. *Genèse de l'Odyssée: le fantastique et le sacré* (Paris, Presses Universitaires de France 1954) 132.

2. *Od.* 10.433.

3. *Od.* 10.283.

4. *Od.* 10.287f.

5. *Od.* 10.292, ἐρέω δὲ ἕκαστα.

6. *Od.* 10.303, καί μοι φύσιν αὐτοῦ ἔδειξε (the only appearance of the word φύσις in Homer).

7. *Od.* 10.279. See especially A. Kirchhoff, *Die Homerische Odyssee* (Berlin 1879) 305f.

8. *Od.* 10.307f.

9. *Od.* 10.337f.

10. *Od.* 10.341.

11. *Od.* 10.389f.

12. Fr. Ortoli, *Les contes populaires de l'Ile de Corse* (Paris 1883) 31f.; L. Radermacher, *Die Erzählungen der Odyssee: Sitzungsberichte der Kais. Akad. der Wissenschaften in Wien, Phil.-Hist. Klasse*, 178 (1916) 9.

13. Grimm, *Kinder-und Hausmärchen* 60. Cf. J. Harrison, *Myths of the Odyssey* (1882) 63f.; J. Bolte and G. Polívka, *Anmerkungen zu den Kinder- und Hausmärchen der Brüder Grimm* (Leipzig 1913) 2.69.

14. *Kathá Sagit Ságara, or, Ocean of the Streams of Story, Translated from the Original Sanskrit by C. H. Tawney* (Calcutta, Baptist Mission Press 1880) 1.337f.; 21,500 couplets by Somadeva, early twelfth century, based on a lost work perhaps as early as the first or second century. Cf. Monro, *Homer's Odyssey XIII–XXIV, Appendix*, p. 292.

15. *Ancient Near Eastern Texts*, ed. J. B. Pritchard (Princeton, 2nd ed. 1955) VI 42f.; cf. Germain, *Genèse de l'Odyssée* 267f.

16. *Od.* 12.3f.

17. *The Thousand and One Nights, Commonly Called in English 'The Arabian Nights Entertainments'*, trans. E. W. Lane, Night 510. Cf. Seeliger, *Myth. Lex.* 2.1195f.; Germain, *Genèse de l'Odyssée* 249f.

18. Cf. *Od.* 5.370f.

19. Cf. *Od.* 10.212f.

20. Cf. *Od.* 10.275f.

21. Cf. *Od.* 10.348f.

22. Cf. *Od.* 10.365.

23. Cf. *Od.* 10.320f.

24. *An Epitome of the History of Ceylon, Compiled from Native Annals; and the First Twenty Chapters of the Mahawamso, Translated by the Hon. George Turnour* (Ceylon, Cotta Church Mission Press

1836) ch. 7, p. 51f. Cf. Rohde, *Gr, Roman*³ 184; Crooke, *Folk-Lore* 19 (1908) 179; Radermacher, *Erzählungen* 8; Weber, *Abh. d. k. Akad. d. Wiss. Berlin* (1870) 15f.; Jügl, *Verh. d. Würzb. Philol.-Vers.* (1868) 58f.

25. Cf. *Od.* 10.307, Ἑρμείας ἀπέβη πρὸς μακρὸν Ὄλυμπον.

26. Cf. *Od.* 10.221f., Κίρκης δ' ἔνδον ἄκουον ἀειδούσης ὀπὶ καλῆι / ἱστὸν ἐποιχομένης.

27. Cf. *Od.* 10.241, ὣς οἱ μὲν κλαίοντες ἐέρχατο.

28. Cf. *Od.* 10.321f., ἄορ ὀξὺ ἐρυσσάμενος ... Κίρκηι ἐπῆιξα ὥς τε κτάμεναι μενεαίνων

29. Cf. *Od.* 10.325f.

30. Cf. *Od.* 10.342f., εἰ μή μοι τλαίης γε, θεά, μέγαν ὅρκον ὀμόσσαι.

31. Boisacq, *Dict. Étym. s.v.* μῶλυ; LSJ *s.v.*; Frisk, *Gr. Etym. Wörterbuch* 2 (1970) 282, is sceptical as usual: 'Fremdwort unbekannter Herkunft'.

32. *Ancient Near Eastern Texts*, p. 103f.; Germain, *Genèse de l'Odyssée* 263f.

33. Frazer, *Balder the Beautiful*, 2.63f.

34. Frazer, *Folk-Lore in the Old Testament*, 2.375f.

35. Aelian *NA* 14.27, paraphrased.

36. *Kathá Sagit Ságara*, 12.71; 2.167f. (Tawney) (see n. 14 above).

37. 'Longinus', περὶ ὕψους 9.14, trans. W. Rhys Roberts, *Longinus: On the Sublime* (Cambridge, 2nd ed. 1907) 69.

38. χοιρίδια κλαίοντα ('Longinus' ibid.). Cf. Aristot. *Meteor.* 1.13; Juvenal 15.13–23.

IV. Aeolus; the Cattle of the Sun; and the Sirens

1. Frazer, *The Golden Bough* (2nd ed. 1911) 1.319f.; cf. L. Radermacher, *Die Erzählungen der Odyssee: Sitzungsberichte der Kais. Akad. der Wissenschaften in Wien, Phil.-Hist. Klasse*, 178 (1916) 18f.; Stith Thompson, *Motif-Index of Folk-Literature* (Helsinki 1932–1934) D 2142.

2. Frazer, *The Golden Bough* 1.319f., from G. M. Dawson, *On the Haida Indians of the Queen Charlotte Islands* (Geological Survey of Canada: Report of Progress for 1878–9) 124 n.

3. Ventris and Chadwick, *Documents in Mycenaean Greek* (Cambridge 1956) 200.

4. Frazer, *The Golden Bough* 1.326. Cf. Crooke, *Folk-Lore* 19 (1908) 185; Kahle, *Zeitschr. d. Vereins für Volkskunde* 10 (1900) 200.

5. J. Grimm, *Teutonic Mythology, Translated from the Fourth Edition by J. S. Stallybrass* (London 1880) 2.640, 4.1473f.; from Glanvil or Bartholomaeus Anglicus, *de proprietatibus rerum* 15.172.

6. K. Müllenhoff, *Sagen, Märchen, und Lieder der Herzogthümer Schleswig Holstein und Lauenburg* (Kiel 1845) no. 301, p. 222. The three knots are similarly employed in no. 308, p. 225.

7. Frazer, *The Golden Bough* 1.326, from C. Leemius, *de Lapponibus Finmarchiae etc. commentatio* (Copenhagen 1767) 454.

8. Frazer, *The Golden Bough* 1.327.

9. Diogenes Laertius 8.60; Empedocles was therefore nicknamed κωλυσανέμας.

10. Radermacher, *Erzählungen* 23f.; Jessen, *RE* 8 (1912) 83f.

11. These lines, 12.374–390, provided A. Kirchhoff (*Die Homerische Odyssee* 293f.) with the foundation of his theory that the greater part of *Od.* 10 and 12 represents a third-person narrative transformed into a first-person narrative. Cf. pp. 55–56 above.

12. *Hymn. Apoll.* 410f.

13. Herodotus 9.93.1, ἔστιν ἐν τῆι Ἀπολλωνίηι ταύτηι ἱρὰ Ἡλίου πρόβατα.

14. Servius on Virg. *Ecl.* 6.60. The theft of the cattle of Apollo is the principal theme of the Homeric *Hymn to Hermes*.

15. Herodotus 9.120. Cf. Radermacher, *Erzählungen* 25. A species of the same genus is to be seen in *Od.* 20.348, αἱμοφόρυκτα δὲ δὴ κρέα ἤσθιον; see S. H. Butcher and A. Lang, *The Odyssey of Homer Done into English Prose* p. 421, n. 17.

16. Plut. *Life of Pyrrhus* 31.

17. Cf. O. Keller, *Die antike Tierwelt* (Leipzig 1909) 368f.

18. J. A. Dubois, *Hindu Manners, Customs, and Ceremonies; Translated by H. K. Beauchamp* (Oxford 1897) 1.193f.; cf. Frazer, *The Golden Bough* 8.35f.

19. H. Jantzen, *Saxo Grammaticus: die ersten neun Bücher der dänischen Geschichte* (Berlin 1900) 447f.; Radermacher, *Erzählungen* 24. There can be no direct relationship between Saxo and Homer, and I agree with Radermacher that indirect relationship is unlikely. Jantzen notes: 'unmittelbare Entlehnung wird nicht vorliegen, wohl aber ist das Motiv in die abenteuerliche Reiseliteratur überhaupt übergegangen, zu der unsere junge Sage gehört'.

20. On 'Siren' (a word of unknown origin) see Weicker, *Der*

Seelenvogel in der antiken Literatur und Kunst (Leipzig 1902), and *Myth. Lex.* 4.601f., with literature; E. Kunze, *Athen. Mittheil.* 57 (1932) 124f.; D. Levi, *AJA* 49 (1954) 280 f.; Radermacher, *Erzählungen* 21f.; C. Robert, *Die Griechische Heldensage* (Berlin 1923) 1365, n. 2; E. Buschor, *Die Musen des Jenseits* (Munich 1944); J. R. T. Pollard, *CR* n.s. 2 (1952) 60 f.

21. Dickens, *Martin Chuzzlewit*, ch. 4.

22. Eur. *Andr.* 936, κλύουσα τούσδε Σειρήνων λόγους . . . ἐξηνεμώθην μωρίαι; Aeschin. 3.228, οὐ κηλεῖσθαί φησι τοὺς ἀκροωμένους ἀλλ' ἀπόλλυσθαι, διόπερ οὐδ' εὐδοκιμεῖν τὴν τῶν Σειρήνων μουσικήν.

23. So already in the seventh century Alcman PMG 30, ἁ Μῶσα κέκλαγ', ἁ λίγηα Σηρήν; 1.96, τᾶν Σηρηνίδων ἀοιδοτέρα κτλ.; cf. Pind. *Parth.* 2.13, σειρῆνα δὲ κόμπον . . . μιμήσομ' ἀοιδαῖς; Alex. Aetol. 7.3, ἀλλ' ὅ τι γράψαι, τοῦτ' ἂν μέλιτος καὶ Σειρήνων ἐτετεύχει; anon. PMG 936.6, ἔνθεον σειρῆνα χεύει; Lucian *de domo* 13, ὑπὸ . . . Σειρῆνος τῶι κάλλει ἑλκόμενος.

24. First in Hesiod, fr. 27 M.-W., Θελξιόπη ἢ Θελξινόη, Μόλπη, Ἀγλαόφωνος; on the red-figure vase reproduced in *Myth Lex.* 4.605, Ἱμερόπα. Cf. Zwicker, *RE* 3A (1927) 291f., *s.v.* 'Sirenen', *Myth. Lex.* 4.603.

25. Soph. fr. 861, with Pearson's note.

26. Ovid *Metam.* 5.552, *Acheloïdes*; Paus. 9.34.2, Σειρῆνας . . . Ἀχελώιου θυγατέρας; Apollod. *Bibl.* 1.7.2.

27. Eur. *Hel.* 167f., πτεροφόροι νεάνιδες, / παρθένοι Χθονὸς κόραι, / Σειρῆνες, εἴθ' ἐμοῖς γόοις / μόλοιτ' ἔχουσαι Λίβυν / λωτὸν κτλ.

28. Apollodorus *Bibl.* 1.7.10, Στερόπη, ἐξ ἧς καὶ Ἀχελώιου Σειρῆνας γενέσθαι λέγουσιν.

29. Details in *Myth. Lex.* 4.604.

30. [Aristot.] *mirab. ausc.* 103; Steph. Byz., *s.v.* Σειρηνοῦσσαι; Strabo C 247.

31. Apollodorus *Epit.* 7.19, ἦν δὲ αὐταῖς Σειρῆσι λόγιον τελευτῆσαι νεὼς παρελθούσης.

32. Lycophron 713f.; cf. Hyginus *Fab.* 124, 141.

33. *Orph. Argon.* 1288f. For a different version of their death, see Steph. Byz. *s.v.* Ἄπτερα: the Sirens, worsted by the Muses in a singing-contest, τὰ πτερὰ τῶν ὤμων ἀπέβαλον καὶ λευκαὶ γενόμεναι εἰς τὴν θάλασσαν ἀνέβαλον ἑαυτάς.

34. E. Kunze, *Athen. Mittheil.* 57 (1932) 124f.; Doro Levi, *AJA* 49 (1945) 280f.; *Myth. Lex.* 4.604f.; *RE s.v.* 'Sirenen' 293f.

35. Soph. fr. 861 P., θροοῦντε τοὺς "Αιδου νόμους; Eur. *Hel.* 167f. (see n. 27 above). These are the two principal literary reflections of the real (not Homeric) Sirens.

36. Cf. Hesiod fr. 27 M.-W., νῆσον ἐς ἀνθεμόεσσαν, of the Sirens (where, as in Ap. Rhod. 4.892, ἀνθεμ. is commonly taken to be a place name).

37. Plato *Cratylus* 403D.

38. The soul itself may be depicted in Siren form: *Myth. Lex.* 4.609; Beazley, *ARVP*² 2.1114–1115, with literature. Cf. R. Weisshäupl, *Grabgedichte der griechischen Anthologie (Abh. Arch. Sem. d. Univ. Wien* 7.1889) 81f.

39. See especially the vase-painting reproduced in *Myth. Lex.* 4.605 (= Beazley, *ARVP*² 1.289, Pfuhl, *Malerei und Zeichnung der Griechen* fig. 479); cf. Robert, *Gr. Heldensage* 1365, n. 2; Zwicker, *RE s.v.* 'Sirenen' 295f.

40. Crooke, *Folk-Lore* 19 (1908) 169f.; Radermacher, *Erzählungen* 21f.; cf. Frazer, *Pausanias* 5.171.

41. *The Indian Antiquary* 10 (1881) 291f.

42. A. Featherman, *Social History of the Races of Mankind: Second Division: Papuo and Malayo Melanesians* (London 1887) 396.

43. K. Bartsch, *Sagen, Märchen, und Gebräuche aus Mecklenburg: 1. Sagen und Märchen* (Wien 1879) no. 545, p. 394. Cf. Stith Thompson, *The Types of Folktale* (Helsinki, 2nd revision 1961) 316, p. 111, and *Motif-Index of Folk-Literature* (Helsinki 1932–1933) F 420, 1.5.2.

44. Crooke, *Folk-Lore* 19 (1908) 170f.

45. *Mélusine: Recueil de Mythologie . . .* 2 (Paris 1884–1885) 280.

46. *Zeitschr. d. Vereins für Volkskunde* 19 (1909) 310. For Sirens in Eddic mythology, see *The Mythology of All Races,* ed. L. H. Gray and G. F. Moore (Boston 1916–1932) 2.210f.

47. *The Jātaka, or Stories of the Buddha's Former Births, Translated from the Pāli by Various Hands under the Editorship of Professor E. B. Cowell,* I (Cambridge 1895) 233f. Cf. *The Indian Antiquary* 10 (1881) 291f.; S. Beal, *Si-yu-ki: Buddhist Records of the Western World* (London 1884) 2.240f.

48. A few of the numerous versions which I have seen may depend ultimately on the *Odyssey;* the majority manifestly do not.

49. For the sake of simplicity I have spoken throughout in terms of the *Odyssey,* though I was long ago persuaded by K. Meuli (*Odyssee und Argonautika*) that the *Odyssey* has taken some of these tales (notably Circe, the Laestrygonians, the Wandering Rocks,

and also the Sirens) from an earlier *Argonautica*. In general, the blend of saga and folktale was certainly found in the pre-Homeric *Argonautica* (attested by *Od.* 12.70), and may go much further back; see L. A. Stella, *Il poema di Ulisse* (Florence 1955) 128f., 169f.

50. Like the females in the story from the *Jātaka*.

51. Again like the *Jātaka* females.

52. *Od.* 12.168f.

53. Cf. Rohde, *Psyche, Translated from the Eighth Edition by W. B. Hillis* (London 1925, reprinted 1950) 593.

54. Milton, *Paradise Lost* 1.781f.

55. For the Siren from Praisos, see J. P. Droop, *BSA* 12 (1905–1906) 41ff.; dated in the end of the eleventh century B.C. by E. Kunze, *Athen. Mittheil.* 57 (1932) 124f., vigorously refuted by Doro Levi, *AJA* 49 (1945) 280 f. For the clay-sealing 'Scylla', see Evans, *BSA* 9 (1902–1903) 58; F. Studniczka, *Athen. Mittheil.* 31 (1906) 50 f.; Evans, *Palace of Minos* 4.952; identified as a hippopotamus by Marinatos, *Deltion* 11 (1927–1928) 53f., followed by A. W. Persson, *New Tombs at Dendra near Midea* (Lund 1942) 184f., and by M. P. Nilsson, *The Minoan-Mycenean Religion and Its Survival in Greek Religion* (Lund, 2nd ed. 1950) 34f. For the 'Scylla' on the siege-rhyton, see Evans, *Palace of Minos* 3.89, Persson 184f., and Nilsson 34f.; she is perhaps wholly an illusion.

Appendix.   The Arrow and the Axes

1. νάσσω means 'pile', 'heap up' (ἔνησε, ἐσώρευσε Schol.) in all the other places where it occurs: Ar. *Eccl.* 840, (Hippocr.) *nat. puer.* 24, Theocr. 9.9, Hippolochus (saec. iv–iii) *ap.* Athen. 4.130 B, cf. Alciphron 3.11.4 (Benner). If you wanted to say 'heap down', 'press down', or the like, the verb was κατανάσσω (Hdt. 7.36, cf. συννάσσω, Reiske's conjecture in Hdt. 7.60). I follow Gow and Scholfield in reading μάξαι (cod. R) for νάξαι (rell.) in Nicander *Ther.* 952. I know no evidence for the sense 'press, squeeze down, stamp down' assigned to this passage by LSJ and by convention, earlier than Arrian *anab.* 6.24.4; though it must be admitted that the one sense might easily pass into the other. The adj. ναστός, 'heaped', seems to have been used in the sense 'solid' (as opposed to 'spongy') by Empedocles and Leucippus (*Vorsokr.*, Index *s.v.*), apparently also by Democritus and by (Hippocr.) *gland.* 16; hence

presumably the use of ναστός as a kind of non-spongy cake, Pherecr. fr. 108.5, Ar. *Av.* 567, *Plut.* 1142, Metagenes fr. 6.3, Diphilus fr. 46, Lycophron 640.

2. Cf. *Od.* 9.391, quoted by Stanford, *CR* 63 (1949) 3ff.; *Od.* 5.234 is a less convincing example (though πέλεκυς is followed by a separate mention of its handle, στειλειόν, it is the πέλεκυς, the axe as a whole, which is ἄρμενον ἐν παλάμῃσι).

3. For the gender-variation without sense-variation, a longish list of examples might be quoted (ἄκρη ἄκρον, δρεπάνη δρέπανον, κοίτη κοῖτος, *al.*).

4. Schol. *ad loc.* (p. 299 Wendel) στελεῆι· τῆι λαβῆι.

5. Cod. *Π* has the more commonplace στειλειόν, rightly rejected by Gow and Scholfield.

6. Schol. V on *Od.* 21.422, ἀπὸ πρώτης γὰρ ὀπῆς τῶν πελέκεων διηνεκῶς ἦλθεν; Schol. H on 19.578, δηλονότι διαβιβάσει τοῦτο εἰς τὰς τρύπας τῶν πελέκεων; Schol. A on *Il.* 23.851, οὕστινας ἐφεξῆς ἱστάντες ἐπί τινα βαθμὸν ἐγυμνάζοντο οἱ τοξόται πέμποντες διὰ τῶν τρητῶν αὐτῶν τὸ βέλος, δι᾽ οὗ ἐμβάλλεται αὐτοῖς ὁ στελειὸς (*v.l.* στηλιά); similarly Eustathius 1531.35 and elsewhere. Hence the lexica: Hesych. στειλε(ι)ή·τοῦ πελέκυος ἡ ὀπὴ εἰς ἣν ἐντίθεται τὸ ξύλον; Et. M. 728.53, στειλειά· τὸ τμῆμα τοῦ πελέκεως δι᾽ οὗ τὸ στελεὸν ἐνείρεται, ἣν τρήμην Ἀττικοὶ λέγουσι; Moeris 254.

7. Stanford, 3ff.

8. Aeneas Tacticus 18.10 (p. 42 Schoene) is best left out of the discussion, because of the lacuna (some 30 letters) which precedes στελεὰ ἐμβάλλεται; the following neuter στελεόν suggests that στελεὰ was neuter plural.

Stanford does not strengthen his case by calling Antiphanes an 'irresponsible comic poet' and Apollonius 'often misguided'. Antiphanes was not so irresponsible as to use στειλειά, if it meant 'hole', in a context where the sense depends on its *not* meaning 'hole'; and it would be remarkable if the learned Apollonius made precisely the same mistake.

9. δρύοχοι. In view of the evidence from usage (see below) it is safe to ignore certain aberrations: (a) 'axes' (Et. M.); (b) 'axes with wooden handles' (Schol. V on *Od.* 19.574); (c) 'the holes of iron axes, into which the handle is inserted' (Hesych.); (d) 'rings set on rods fixed in the ground, through which arrows are shot' (Et. M.). We have then to choose between two interpretations, both suitable to *Od.* 19.574:

(i) Stocks, trestles, or the like, a row of blocks or pegs set level in the ground in a straight line, on which the keel was laid at the start of ship-building: Schol. V on 19.574, κυρίως μὲν τοὺς πασσάλους ἐφ᾽ ὧν τὴν τρόπιν ἱστᾶσι τῶν καινουργουμένων πλοίων; Schol. BHQ ibid., ξύλα εἰσὶν ὀρθὰ ὑποκάτω τῆς τρόπιδος κτλ.; Eustathius ad loc., κυρίως πάσσαλοι ἐφ᾽ ὧν στοιχηδὸν διατεθειμένων ἡ τρόπις ἵσταται κτλ.; Schol. Ap. Rhod. 1.723 (p. 60 Wendel), ἐν οἷς καταπήσσεται ἡ τρόπις ξύλοις; Schol. Plat. Timae. 81 B (p. 289 Greene), τὰ στηρίγματα τῆς πηγνυμένης νεὼς δρυόχους φασὶν (= Suid. s.v. ii p. 143 Adler): Et. M. 228.36, ἄμεινον δὲ ἀκούειν δρυόχους ξύλα ὀρθὰ ἐφ᾽ ὧν ἡ τρόπις ἐρείδεται τῆς πηγνυμένης νεώς, ἤγουν στηρίγματα.

(ii) The ribs (already fitted into the keel): Schol. Ap. Rhod. 1.723, δρυόχους οὖν τὰ ἐγκοίλια τῆς νεώς; cf. Schol. BHQ on Od. 19.574, τινὲς δὲ δρυόχους φασὶν τὰ πρῶτα πηγνύμενα ξύλα εἰς ναυπηγίαν; Pollux 1.85 (i p. 27 Bethe) μέρη δὲ νεὼς δρύοχον, τρόπις, κτλ.; Apoll. Soph. 60.23.

The beginning of the entry in Suid., πάτταλοι οἱ ἐντιθέμενοι ναυπηγουμένης νεώς, may be a slightly distorted fragment of the same explanation as that given by Schol. V and Eust. on 19.574 in favour of (i) above.

The former of these alternatives is clearly the favorite, a choice confirmed by the criterion of usage:

(a) δρυόχους τιθέναι when metaphorical means 'lay foundations': Ar. Thesm. 52, δρυόχους τιθέναι δράματος ἀρχάς. If you want to stress the first step in ship-building, you will refer either to the placing of the trestles on which the keel is laid or to the laying of the keel; not to the more advanced stage at which the trestles are in place, the keel laid, and the ribs already attached.

(b) ἐκ δρυόχων metaphorically means '(fresh) from the stocks': Plat. Timae. 81 B, καινὰ τὰ τρίγωνα οἷον ἐκ δρυόχων; the image is of a ship freshly launched from its cradle, and this example is decisive in favor of (i) above. In Polybius 1.38.5, αὖθις ἔγνωσαν ἐκ δρυόχων εἴκοσι καὶ διακόσια ναυπηγεῖσθαι σκάφη, the meaning is plainly 'from the very beginning', and again the sense 'foundation-blocks', 'stocks', is far the more natural.

There is no certain example of the alternative in usage. Procopius Bell. Goth. 4.22 writes ξύλα σύμπαντα ἐς τὴν τρόπιν ἐναρμοσθέντα ἅπερ οἱ μὲν ποιηταὶ δρυόχους καλοῦσι, ἕτεροι δὲ νομέας ('ribs'); this only shows what Procopius thought the word meant in 'the poets'; it is clear that he and his contemporaries did not use the word in that sense. It may, however, be thought that (ii) makes at least as good sense in Plutarch *de fort. Rom.* 321 E (2 ii p. 60 Teubner) οὕτω τὴν ʻΡώμην ὁ μὲν πρῶτος ἄρχων καὶ δημιουρ-γὸς ἐξ ἀγρίων καὶ βοτήρων ὥσπερ ἐκ δρυόχων κραταιῶν συνιστ-άμενος οὐκ ὀλίγους πόνους ἔσχε (the whole context is relevant, from 321 D ὥσπερ γὰρ ὁλκὰς onwards).

The epigram of Archimelus quoted in Athen. 5.209 C, πῶς δὲ κατὰ δρυόχους ἐπάγη σανίς, is indecisive; κατὰ δρυόχους may mean ʻon the stocks' or ʻon the ribs'. Indecisive also is the epigram quoted by Suid., τὸν δ᾿ ἔτι θείης / εὔστοχον ἐν πόντωι, τὸν δὲ κατὰ δρυόχους (if the text were reliable, there would be an obvious contrast between a ship at sea and a ship still ʻon the stocks'). In Ap. Rhod., δρυόχους ἐπεβάλλετο νηός, the sense is uncertain (probably ὑπεβάλλετο should be read).

The conclusion is clear enough. Usage, especially that of the earliest examples, is our sole reliable criterion. We find that the meaning ʻstocks' is certain in Plato, highly probable in Aristophanes, and perfectly appropriate in Polybius. Of the alternative ʻribs' or ʻkeel with ribs', there is no likely example earlier than Plutarch. We shall therefore understand the Odyssean phrase in the sense ʻlike keel-supports'. The axes are planted in a row, forming a straight line, like the blocks set at intervals in a line for the laying of a keel. The points of resemblance are (i) that the objects are spaced at intervals; (ii) that they are all erected to exactly the same height; (iii) that the row is a straight line; and therefore (iv) that, regarded as a whole, the line of axes looks like something on which you might lay the keel of a ship.

10. LSJ *s.v.* πρότερος B I i; Ebeling, *Lex. Hom. s.v.* πρῶτος (2); Hom. *Il.* 6.40, 16.371, 20.275f., 22.66.

11. Quoted by A. D. Fraser, *CW* 26 (1932–1933) 25ff.; I have not yet seen this work of the Comte de Caylus.

12. Helbig, *Hom. Epos* (1887) 348ff.; Monro, *Odyssey* (1901) on 19.571ff.; Butcher and Lang, *Translation*, n. on 19.578; Fraser, 25ff.

13. Goebel, *N. Jb.* 22 (1876) 169ff.; Lexilogus 1 (1878) 448ff.

14. ʻZu dem Ende musste der Pfeil dicht über das in die Rundung noch mit einem kurzen Stücke hineinragende obere Ende des Stieles einer jeden Axt hinstreifen'; and again ʻder Pfeil streifte bei sämmtlichen Äxten oben den Stiel oder das Stielende'.

15. *Odyssea* (1917), notes on 19.573–579 and (p. 590) on 21.422.

16. In the *Badminton Archery* (Badminton Library of Sports and Pastimes: *Archery*, by C. J. Longman and H. Walrond, 1894) p. 86. See also Wallace McLeod, *AJA* 66 (1962) 13, with references n. 2.

17. *The Book of the Bow* (1958) 35.

18. Ibid. 35–36.

19. Ibid. 217.

20. Longman 428ff.: 'I agree in the main with Mr. Ford's opinion that 300 yards is about as far as the average man can expect to reach, though an archer of exceptional physique can cover another 50 or 60 yards'; Ford shot a little over 300 yards, using a 68-pound bow. Grimley (p. 45, n. 1) reports a distance of 651 yards in California (1957)—presumably with a metal bow.

21. The books abound with yarns, scorned by the champion archers. Most of the alleged feats are as incredible as that of Hiawatha; 'Strong of arm was Hiawatha; / he could shoot the arrows upward, / shoot them with such strength and swiftness / that the tenth had left the bowstring / ere the first to earth had fallen'. The indefatigable Longman could only manage to get the third off the string as the first fell to the ground.

22. *Hunting with Bow and Arrow* (1925), quoted by Grimley 77.

23. Quoted by Longman 428ff.

24. See Longman 107 and 430, Grimley 63, Oman, *Art of War in the Middle Ages*[2] (1953) 119, n. 2. Longman himself shot a steel-tipped arrow at 6–7 yards at a gate of seasoned timber one inch thick; the tip came through on the other side.

25. *Folk-Lore* 19 (1908) 154.

26. *Genèse de l'Odyssée: le fantastique et le sacré* (Paris, Presses Universitaires de France 1954). I had thought that the observations about the parallels of the *Mahābhārata* and *Rāmāyana*, and the remarkable conclusion to be drawn from them, were my own: I am very much obliged to Professor Dodds for referring me to Dr. Germain's book, in which precisely the same parallels and conclusion are drawn, but on much wider and deeper foundations.

27. C. Swynnerton, *Romantic Tales from the Panjab* (1903) 212ff., with illustration.

28. *The Jātaka*, trans. H. T. Francis, V (1905) 68f.

29. From the *Epitome* in the Temple Classics (1898) by Romesch Dutt, sect. 17ff.

30. *Rāmāyana* I i, trans. R. T. Griffiths (*sic*; properly Griffith), in *Hindu Literature* (World's Great Classics 1900) p. 177.

31. Germain quotes other Indian versions, especially the Buddhist hagiography *Lalita Vistara* ('le trait transperce les 5 boucliers, les 7 arbres, le sanglier de fer'). Professor A. T. Hatto has referred me to F. Coxwell, *Siberian and other Folk-Tales* (London 1925): 'The bride said to Aleyka, "What can you do? Show me your powers". He sang this answer, "Upon this isle took thirty poplars root, but all will fall so soon as I shall shoot"... He lifted an arrow and at a shot from his bow thirty black poplars fell; the arrow had cut down twenty-nine of them, and was embedded in the thirtieth tree'. He refers me also to W. Fleischer, *Das Uzbekische Heroische Volks-epos*, in Paul-Braune, *Beitr. z. Gesch. d. deutschen Sprache und Literatur*, Bd. 80 (Ost) 14ff. (the returning hero strings a bow as proof of identity). See now also Wallace E. Mcleod, *AJA* 66 (1962) 13 ('Minamoto Yoshiiye, a Japanese hero of the 11th century, shot through three sets of armour as they hung from a tree'). No doubt the list could be further extended; so far there is nothing much west of India.

32. Germain's book as a whole makes a strong case in favor of this conclusion (which he himself explicitly draws).

33. Olympia: *Olympia* IV (1890) 71, and *Bronzen von Olympia* 470. Sparta: *The Sanctuary of Artemis Orthia at Sparta* (1929) 199. Lousoi: *Jahreshefte d. oest. arch. Inst. in Wien* IV (1901) 49. Delphi: *Fouilles de Delphes* V (1908) 120. Cyprus: G. M. A. Richter, *Greek, Etruscan and Roman Bronzes*, 1935–1936. See also Robinson, *Excav. at Olynthus* X (1941) 341, with bibliography; Reinach in Daremberg-Saglio *s.v. securis*; Blümner, *Technol.* II (1879) 200; *BSA* 6 (1899–1900) 108; Cook, *Zeus* III (1940) 646ff. For a Minoan example (M.M. III/L.M. I), see Marinatos, *Praktika* (1935) 218: the gold votive from Arkalochori shown top left in fig. 19 has a ring near the handle-tip.

34. For a large and convenient assembly see Cook, *Zeus* III (1940) 656ff.

35. Published by Blinkenberg, *Archaeologische Studien* (1904) 31ff. Cf. Reinach fig. 6272. Actual examples with handle-tips rounded or flattened and pierced for suspension have been found at Lousoi, Sparta, and Delphi.

36. Longman 72: if the axes were a yard apart, 'in twelve yards the arrow would only fall 4 inches by gravitation'.

37. So also Fraser 25ff.; he takes θύραζε to mean simply 'out at the other end' (not 'to the door'), quoting *Il.* 21.29, 237, *Od.* 5.410.

38. *SB. d. preuss. Akad. d. Wiss., Phil.-Hist. Klasse* (1935) 186ff.,

approved by Wüst, *RE* 17.2 (1937) 1988: 'in den ligurischen Fels-zeichnungen kommen vielfach Beile vor ... Sie haben meist den langen Stiel des Kriegsbeils und am Stielende regelmässig einen Ring zum Aufhängen'; see Blinkenberg 31ff.

39. 31ff.; Professor Dodds has drawn my attention to the fact that Blinkenberg's explanation is adopted in the tenth edition (1911) of Ameis-Hentze-Cauer's *Odyssee* (on 19.574). I confess that I had not consulted that edition, only earlier and later ones in which this explanation is not given.

40. Ed. 1726, vol. V, facing p. 49. When I gave this paper as a lecture to a conference at Oxford in 1961 I had not looked at any of the early (illustrated) editions of Pope's translation. I am obliged to Professor H. N. Rydon for a timely reminder (in a letter to the London *Times* dated 11 August 1961). He quotes a 'tailpiece to Book XXI' in the edition of 1760; the first edition has a full-page woodcut ('P. Fourdrinier sculp.', clumsily enough).

41. The significance of this was seen by Blinkenberg 31ff.: δρυόχους· τοὺς πελέκεις· οἱ μὲν κρίκους ἀκούουσί τινας μεγάλους ἐπ' ὀβελίσκων κειμένους, οὓς καταπηγνῦσθαι εἰς τὴν γῆν ὥστε δι' αὐτῶν τοξεύειν.

42. See now Anna Sacconi, *Un Problema di interpretazione omerica; la freccia e le asce del libro XXI dell' Odissea* (Università degli Studi de Roma: Facoltà de Lettere e Filosofia; Rome 1971). She finds support for my interpretation in the Pylos Tablet TA 716, first line, '*pa-sa-ro ku-ru-so a-pi to-ni-jo* 2 *wa-o* *232 2', which she renders 'two well-rounded golden pegs (πάσσαλοι) ... two double axes (*232 = a double axe lying horizontally)'. She takes this to signify pegs on which the axes are to be hung. She also has a new solution for the problem of the ὄγχιον in *Od.* 21.61 (which I had neglected): the common opinion is that the ὄγχιον contained the axes; Anna Sacconi rightly rejects this, and suggests that it contained arrows (or barbed arrow-heads, ὄγχοι). I am very much obliged to Anna Sacconi for her help in this matter.

Index

Index